EIGG, AN ISLAND LANDSCAPE

The dark sands of Laig

Front cover: Galmisdale house and An Sgurr

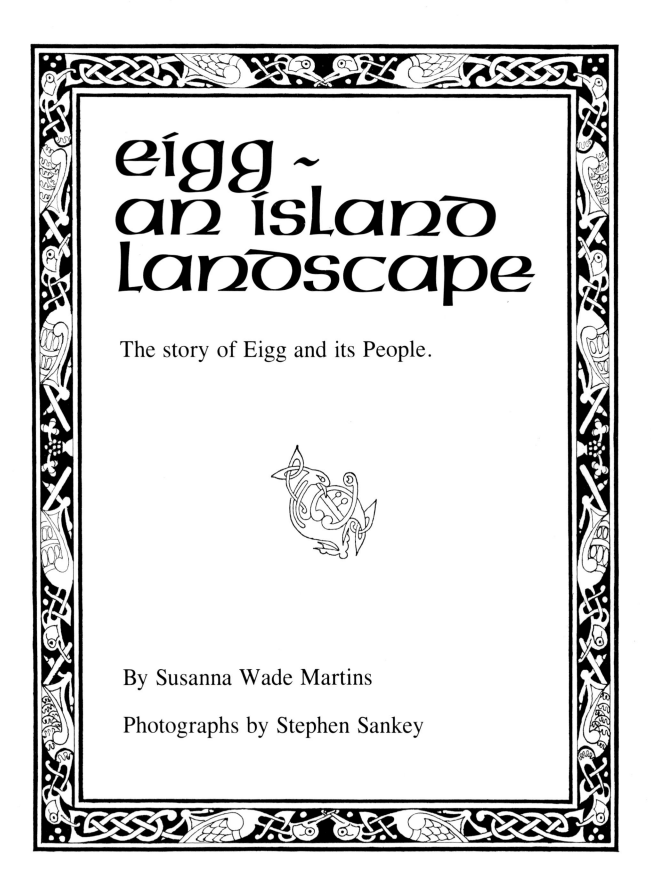

eigg ~ an island landscape

The story of Eigg and its People.

By Susanna Wade Martins

Photographs by Stephen Sankey

COUNTRYSIDE PUBLISHING SCOTLAND

First published in Great Britain by
Countryside Publishing,
Scotland.

©Text 1987 by Susanna Wade Martins
©Photographs 1987 by Stephen Sankey
Typeset in Times by Spire Origination
Printed by Witley Press Ltd., Hunstanton,
Norfolk.

British Library Cataloguing in
Publication Data

Wade Martins, Susanna
Eigg — an island landscape: the story
    of Eigg & its people.
    1. Anthropo-geography—Scotland—Eigg
    2. Eigg—Historical geography
    I. Title II. Sankey, Stephen
    304.2′09411′85   GF556.E/

ISBN 0-9510285-1-0

CONTENTS

'For your added pleasure'

A post and Rhum

ACKNOWLEDGEMENTS

This book has been a pleasure to write because it has been a project involving all my family; my husband, Peter and our two sons, Richard and Edward. We have come to regard Eigg as one of the most beautiful corners of the British Isles.

My publisher, Kate Sankey of Countryside Publishing has given help far beyond the call of duty and her interest and infectious enthusiasm as well as her editorial comments have always been a great encouragement.

The Royal Museum of Scotland provided photographs of objects held by them and found on Eigg which have been used for drawings in this book.

The Society of Antiquaries of Scotland gave permission for the reproduction of drawings of Viking finds from Eigg published in the *Transactions* of the Society. The School of Scottish Studies allowed me to reproduce part of a poem by Hugh MacKinnon published in their journal *Tocher*.

The archaeological survey was sponsored by the Society of Antiquaries of Scotland. The work was carried out by a dedicated team headed by Philip Williams of the Norfolk Archaeological Unit who drew the plans. Line drawings are by Sue White, also of the Norfolk Archaeological Unit, and I am very grateful to other members of the Unit for their general assistance and advice. Other maps and plans were redrawn by Martin Leverington while Anne Campbell of Eigg provided Celtic designs, borders and the maps inside the back and front covers. The photographs were printed by David Miller.

I would also like to thank Keith Schellenberg for his hospitality both at the Lodge when he allowed me to trace the William Bald map of Eigg, and also for providing accommodation for the archaeological survey team.

Many of the people of Eigg have given generously of their time to talk about the island's past as well as its future and I would particularly like to thank Dougal MacKinnon and Duncan Mackay. Duncan Mackay and Dolly Ferguson also lent old photographs some of which are reproduced in the book. Morag MacKinnon at the school allowed me to read the school log books in her comfortable home.

The whole project would have floundered at an early stage if it had not been for the active encouragement of Angus MacKinnon of Cleadale, Eigg, and it is to him that I would like to give particular thanks, firstly for permission to quote from the tapes made by his father for the School of Scottish Studies and secondly for the hours spent pouring over old maps with me explaining the development of the crofts and crofting life. He also searched out old photographs and shared his great knowledge of the island's past. He always makes us welcome and his hospitality is generous. It was his concern that much of the island's history, particularly its oral traditions, would be lost that has resulted in this book.

INTRODUCTION

Eigg and Rhum from Portnaluchaig

The journey to the Isle of Eigg either by road or rail via Fort William to Mallaig, is through some of the most beautiful scenery in Scotland. The West Highland line, built a century ago to move fish, hugs the narrow shore-line between the loch and hills for much of its route north from Fort William to the spectacular viaduct at the head of Loch Shiel. Here, at Glenfinnan the statue of Charles Edward Stewart on its high column watches down the loch to the sea. Heading westwards through rocky hills, the train reaches the coast at Arisaig before turning north along the indented boulder strewn coast for Mallaig.

The narrow winding road frequently runs parallel to the railway, crossing it from time to time, until they both reach the busy little fishing port of Mallaig, always buzzing with activity at midday in the holiday season when the ferries for Skye and the Small Isles (of which Eigg is one) are due to leave. The pier is littered with rucksacks, oilskins and cardboard boxes of groceries while heavy booted hikers wait beside their piles of luggage and supplies, for the ferry to appear. There is an almost daily service to the Small Isles during the summer months either from Mallaig or the smaller jetty further south at Arisaig.

The distinctive profile of Eigg is visible from the mainland for the last part of the journey north. A basalt plateau slopes downwards towards the south and east with vertical cliffs dropping to the sea. To the west are the majestic columnar rocks of An Sgurr, rising 400 metres above sea level and jutting up above the plateau surface like the funnel of some giant ocean liner.

The crossing takes up to an hour and a half and the first close view of the island is of steep forbidding cliffs, a haven for birds, but a danger to shipping. The ferry heads for a gap in the rock wall where flatter land, following a fault line slopes down to two sandy bays. The substantial white-washed buildings of Kildonnan farm on the green promontory overlooking the bay are the first sign of habitation. Here it was that St Donan founded his monastery some 1300 years ago, bringing Christianity from Ireland. Measuring roughly four miles by six, much of Eigg is barren basalt moor; yet it has a varied and fascinating landscape, created partly by geology and climate, and partly by man.

By the shore to the south are a few buildings around the harbour. The tea rooms and the estate office with their strange castellations were built in the 1930s by the island's then owner, Sir Walter Runciman. Unlike most of the rest of the island, this sheltered south-east coast is wooded; most of the trees were planted about a century ago by one of the island's previous owners. The harbour is sheltered from the south by the small, uninhabited Castle Island which is now used as summer pasture for the estate rams after shearing. In harder times this flat, but rocky, island was covered with cultivation strips, or 'lazy beds'. When the population was high and land was scarce, it was worth working even this barren outcrop for the small numbers of potatoes it could produce. Now there is only a lighthouse and a tall monument to one of the island's more eccentric proprietors who chose to be buried there in splendid isolation in 1913.

The larger ferries cannot enter the shallow harbour and so travellers, along with the essential stores and the odd pig or goat, have to be picked up by a motor boat for the final part of the long journey. There is always a small crowd on the pier when the boat arrives, waiting to meet returning friends and visitors. The van from the post office collects mail and stores while others gather simply because they know that it is a sure meeting place for the exchange of news and information.

Many visitors to the island come only for a few hours and will be picked up later in the day by the returning ferry. Some of these, particularly if the weather is wet and wild, will not get much further than the tea rooms, while others attracted by the famous 'singing sands' will want to cross the island to Cleadale in the north-west and find Camas Sgiotaig (singing sands bay). Making this four-mile journey by foot, by bike hired at the pier, or in an island vehicle, they will follow the road as it rises slowly beside the wood and then come out on open ground. Much of this higher ground was cultivated 150 years ago but now is covered with heather and bracken with only part of it improved grazing for sheep.

Above the road as it rises up from the sea is the woodland around Eigg Lodge, the home of the island's proprietor who farms this side of the island. A different world of lush lawns, rhododendrons and even a few palm trees greets the sightseer who crosses the cattle grid which separates the genteel home and gardens from the harsh reality of the rest of the island.

Passing the church, school and shop, the road follows the depression across the centre of the island between the heather-clad slopes and a small area of recent afforestation. Always to the west is the great pitchstone mass of An Sgurr, often shrouded in low cloud or mist. Just past the middle of the island, the road begins to descend, and suddenly, ahead across the sea is the first dramatic view of the island of Rhum with its barren rocky coast and mountain peaks. Recent excavations have shown this unlikely outpost to have been the home of the earliest men yet found in Scotland. The road now bends sharply at the head waters of Allt a' Bhealaich Chlithe and the descent into Cleadale begins. Lower down, the winding road is bordered by the small squat stone houses so typical of the crofts of north-west Scotland. The nearer group, at Chuagach all date from a resettlement of the 1890s when the Lodge was built and families were moved. Further on, enclosed by a dramatic 300 metre high amphitheatre of vertical pitchstone, is Cleadale itself; the houses are often older but of the same simple style. It is clear that this is an area very different to the south-east of the island: this is the crofting community with its small houses and walled enclosures, but few of the crofts are still worked. Cattle, the traditional livestock of the crofters, along with goats, a more recent introduction, can be seen. The area has a neglected air. Disused cars and machinery are left about for the brambles to climb over. Bracken is encroaching fast on the abandoned upper fields, and rushes are taking over in the lowlands. Walls are broken and barbed wire slack and ineffective.

Between the occupied cottages are several ruined ones and this feeling of neglect and abandonment is something that visitors from the intensely farmed south of Britain find very hard to accept. The few tilled fields are a welcome reminder that with hard work and determination, the rich black soils can be drained and made to produce good crops.

Beyond the crofts is the wide sweep and grey sands of Laig Bay. The singing sands are reached along a track running north through the area of common grazing first enclosed by the crofters shortly after 1810. Rising up to the almost vertical wall of rock are the straight and parallel walls separating the individual holdings of the crofts. All this land is now abandoned and most of the walls are broken. The track then descends along the cliff to the singing sands and it is here that, if they are dry, the grey granite sands under the cliffs 'sing', or more accurately, squeak, as they are walked on.

Even this single excursion gives a clear, if rather rushed idea of the variety of landscape and history to be found on this small island. More strenuous is the climb up An Sgurr. Branching left behind the pier another track follows the edge of pasture sheltered by mature woodland, past the estate farm at Galmisdale and out onto open moorland, much of which was once cultivated. On the south of the track at the top of a rise is a small cairn on the site of a much older one which is said to have been built by the mourners in the funeral cortege of a famous piper from Grulin, Donald MacQuarrie. Here the cortege waited for the arrival of the chief mourner, Ronald Macdonald, a piper from Arisaig and the teacher of Donald. He landed at the bay next to the harbour and played his pipe all the way to Garbh Bealach where the cairn was being built. He then led the funeral party to the burial ground at Kildonnan.

Music has always played a very large part in island life, perhaps partly inspired by the ever present sound of the wind and the waves, but only on Eigg is there a knoll, Cnoc-na-piobaireachd (near Grulin) where new tunes could be learnt on a beautiful moonlit night by putting an ear to the ground and just listening.

Various paths lead off around the back of An Sgurr, up through boulders and scree and on to the top. The view, described by Macdonald in 1811 as 'yielding scenes unparalleled in Britain', includes the mountains of the mainland and Skye, the small island of Muck to the south-west and on a clear day far out to sea, the black humps of the Outer Hebrides. Below is a fairy-tale landscape of mountains and lochs; yet even here, in an area that can never have been hospitable to man, there are the remains of human activity. On the top of An Sgurr is a prehistoric fort, and lower down in one of the lochs is a small island defence or 'dun', further evidence of prehistoric settlement. To the west, below An Sgurr, between the mountain wall and the sea, is a green and fertile strip of land where there were once two townships: Upper and Lower Grulin. Forcibly evicted in 1853, most of the inhabitants were shipped to Nova Scotia. The ruins of their houses, some standing almost to roof level, can still be seen in this, one of the most beautiful corners of the island – ruins which are monuments to the disastrous social consequences of 19th century agricultural changes in much of northern Scotland.

There is far more to be seen on this island than can possibly be explored in one visit. Those who are privileged to spend longer here want to return again and again. Islands have a magnetism all of their own and inspire a unique type of community life in which there is much to admire.

However, there is sadness here that even the most casual visitor cannot fail to sense. The

Ceilidh band at Hogmanay

population of sixty, only one tenth of its mid-nineteenth century peak, continues to decline. The problems of farming such a remote and inaccessible island, and of selling its produce are disheartening. The sight of overgrown fields and abandoned farms gives no pleasure, but reflects the almost insuperable odds that modern technology and society have stacked against little communities such as that on Eigg.

On the return trip to the mainland, the excited anticipation of the outward journey has been replaced by a subdued thoughtfulness; the island and possible solutions to the problems facing its small community are discussed. The only point on which all the travellers are agreed is that somehow island ways of life in their beautiful surroundings, divorced from many of the man-made strains of modern society, must be helped to survive in this competitive and materialistic world.

Any future must be built on a knowledge of the past and few groups of people can be more conscious of their traditions and their history than these Gaelic island communities. This short book frequently calls upon those traditions to explain how the island has come to be as it is today. The economic problems are obvious, but I leave it to others to suggest solutions.

IN THE BEGINNING

An Sgurr and the graves of Sir William Peterson and family and Dr MacAskill of Kildonnan

We do not know when men first settled on Eigg. The last ice sheets of the Pleistocene period finally retreated from Scotland in about 9,000 B.C. and as the climate improved, settlers moved north. There was little flint to be found in the western Highlands and Islands, but bloodstone, an attractive red flecked stone found at Bloodstone Hill on Rhum, and as pebbles on the beaches, could have been used for implements. The earliest evidence for man in Scotland has been found near Kinloch Castle on Rhum where a site dating from about 6,500 B.C. is currently being excavated. As well as the bloodstone implements, botanical remains such as hazel nuts show that by this time the climate was warm enough to support woodland of birch and hazel in the area. These people were hunters, fishers and gatherers and left little sign of their dwellings, which were probably only temporary shelters. On Eigg, the evidence for Stone Age man has been mostly chance finds: an arrowhead in a field near Kildonnan, a stone axe found in 1889 'on a road crossing Eigg' and a polished stone axe from Cleadale. Various implements including another polished axe come from within a cairn containing two box-like coffins made of flat stones which were uncovered in 1853 just below Laig farm. These polished implements all date from the New Stone Age, thought to begin about 3,000 B.C. in Scotland.

The custom of burying the dead in stone coffins or 'cists' built of flat stones under a cairn is usually associated with the New Stone Age or early Bronze Age; the period in which henges and solitary standing stones were erected. No standing stones have yet been found on Eigg, although there is a tantalisingly vague reference to 'two circles of stones' and 'several stone monuments' in an article about the antiquities of Eigg, written in 1878. On the lower slopes of An Sgurr above Grulin are two newly discovered structures, each consisting of a standing stone, one now fallen, each surrounded by a circular wall. (grid reference NM459844). There are several mounds or stone cairns near the coast, some containing cists. These areas of flat fertile land near Laig, Kildonnan and Grulin were suitable for primitive cultivation and close to shallow bays ideal for beaching boats.

Another group of possibly five cairns has recently been identified in the area of highland and lochs to the north of An Sgurr near Lochan Nighean Dughaill. It is difficult to suggest an explanation for this very remote location (NM452859).

One socketed bronze axe, now in the Royal Museum of Scotland and found somewhere near Kildonnan, is the only other evidence for occupation throughout the entire period from about 1,600 to 400 B.C.

From about the eighth century B.C. it seems that major changes were taking place in Scottish society. Stone-walled hill forts were built, indicating a period of conflict between incoming and older inhabitants. Some of these invasions came from further south where firstly Belgic and then later the Roman incursions were disrupting life and resulting in a movement northwards. By the first century B.C. a great variety of smaller hillforts or 'duns' were being erected in highland Scotland and it is about this time that the very distinctive tower forts known as 'brochs' began to appear in the Western Isles. There are no brochs on the Small Isles, although there are several on Skye. Presumably this is because the population was too small to build them. Instead, sites on Eigg which were naturally well defended were improved to form duns or forts. One of these, of which there is now very little to be seen, surrounded the area where the buildings at the pier now stand. This rocky promontory overlooking the bay was an obvious point to protect against invaders. The defences consisted of a circular wall with a diameter of about 30 metres in which natural outcrops of stone were incorporated, but it is now bisected by the modern road.

A second fort, occupying a similar promontory site was built at Kildonnan; here parts of a turf-covered wall enclosing a triangular area can be clearly seen. This is said to be the site of St Donan's later monastery, so the earthworks within the fort may well belong to both periods.

As well as these coastal defences, there are two very remote fortified island retreats. In one of the many lochs in the high moorland overlooked by An Sgurr is a small defended island or dun with a low wall around it (NM456853). It could only have held a very few defenders, being only about 14 by eight metres, but it would certainly have been very difficult to attack.

Another very good defensive site was the top of An Sgurr itself, where a much larger fort, covering about four hectares was built. On all sides, except the west, the approach was up a 150 metre sheer cliff of pitchstone; only on the west were any man-made defences needed. Here a wall about 80 metres long was built, blocking the only means of entry up a steep and difficult

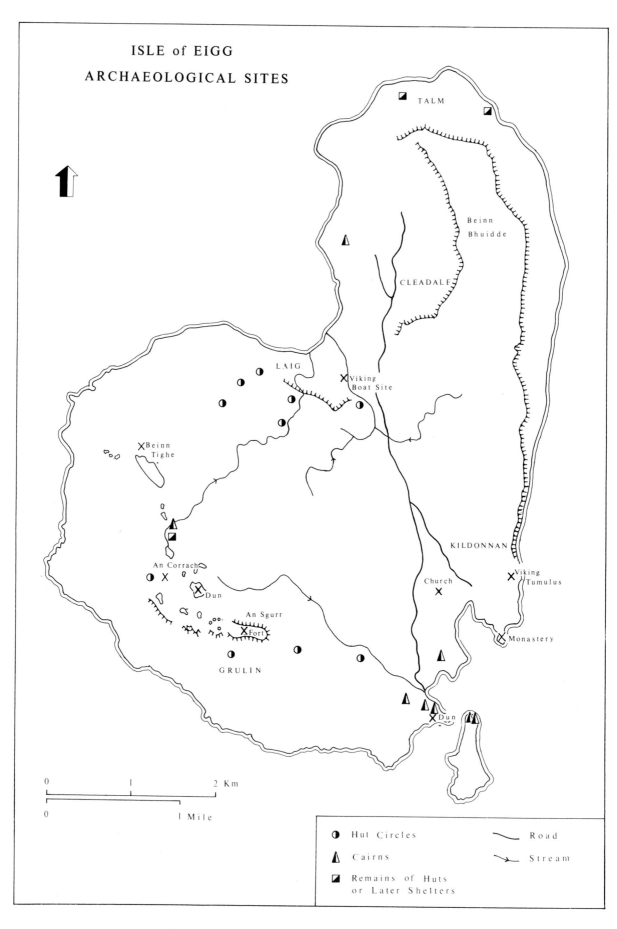

ISLE of EIGG
ARCHAEOLOGICAL SITES

TALM

Beinn
Bhuidde

CLEADALE

LAIG

Viking
Boat Site

Beinn
Tighe

KILDONNAN

An Corrach

Church

Viking
Tumulus

Dun

An Sgurr

Fort

Monastery

GRULIN

Dun

0   1   2 Km

0   1 Mile

Hut Circles   Road

Cairns   Stream

Remains of Huts
or Later Shelters

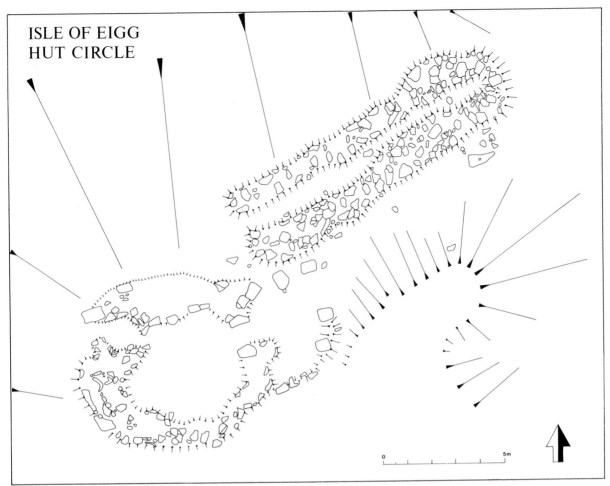

ISLE OF EIGG
HUT CIRCLE

This circular stone walled hut above Laig farm (NM460863) is well preserved. Two entrances opposite each other can clearly be seen to the east and west. There is some sign of a 'porch' around the eastern entrance, and to the north-east is a long, narrow stone walled structure, but its purpose is unclear.

The map opposite shows some of the more impressive and easily accessible archaeological sites on the island, all of which provide a varied and beautiful hill walk.

These include a climb up the steep path behind Laig farm to look for hut circles on the hill sides.

A walk along the path from Galmisdale and up An Squrr where the remains of the Iron Age defensive wall can be seen on the west side of the summit.

A hike onto An Corrach and the wilds of Beinn Tighe via the island dun in loch nam Ban Mora.

A search around the Kildonnan shoreline for the old fort monastery and cairns.

Flint arrowhead.

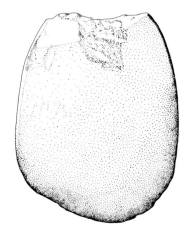

Part of a polished stone axe.

Bronze socketed axe head.

A selection of finds from Eigg, now in the Royal Museum of Scotland.

slope. Much of this wall has collapsed, but in places, particularly at its northern end, it stands to between one and two metres high.

In none of these duns or forts is there any clear indication of permanent occupation, but in other places on the island, there are remains of hut circles where the inhabitants would have lived, retreating to the forts in times of danger. In the summer, it can be very difficult to find these circles in the bracken and it is not easy to distinguish them amidst the many natural boulders which litter the moorland. However, some are clearly visible, particularly above Laig farm, overlooking Laig bay. That these circles survive only in remote and difficult positions suggests that those on more hospitable sites have been robbed of their stones over the centuries. These hut sites can be identified as circles of boulders, sometimes piled up two or three courses high. There is usually an entrance, and often a walled enclosure on one side. The huts vary in size from about seven to ten metres in diameter, and the adjacent walled enclosures suggest that animals were kept. Nowhere is there evidence of nearby cultivation contemporary with the huts.

In the rugged land to the north of An Sgurr at the head of the small valley of the Abhainn Gleann Charadail is a series of very strange constructions (NM452856). They are tiny huts built of the blocks of pitchstone in the valley floor, with roofs corbelled inwards. They are difficult to find amongst the stones of the valley floor and might have been used for hiding, as they are far too small to have been occupied for any length of time. It is very unlikely that the only areas of the island occupied in the pre-historic periods were the marginal lands where the hut circles now survive. However, they are evidence that over the thousand years up to the Viking period a significant number of people were living on Eigg. Whether the remote upland hut circles represent permanent homes, or whether they were used only in the summer as temporary shelters, or 'shielings', when live-stock was driven to the higher ground, is impossible to say. They are difficult to date and it is quite likely that they continued to be used into more modern times as seasonal dwellings.

Until the fifth century all Scotland was under the control of the Picts, a name, which means 'painted people' given to them by the Romans. Before the sixth century there were several independent tribes, but by 500 A.D. they had been amalgamated into only two, the North and South Picts, divided by the Great Glen. These

An Sgurr: Iron Age defensive wall

people were probably not newcomers, but were descended from the Iron Age and Bronze Age inhabitants of the area.

From the fifth century a new group of Gaelic speaking peoples from Ireland, known as 'Scots', began to settle in what is now Argyll, and their kingdom of Dalriada came into being covering both Argyll and some of the Western Isles. Between the fifth and ninth centuries there was continued rivalry between the North and South Picts and Dalriada. Finally, in the 850s the Dalriaden king, Kenneth MacAlpin ruled all Scotland except for the areas under Norse control. This Dalriaden domination was partly the result of conquest and partly the result of amalgamations brought about by marriage.

Eigg was probably on the margins of the area of Pictish and Scottish control and its importance to either kingdom would have been as a convenient harbourage and source of supplies for vessels coming from the southern Hebrides to Skye or from the mainland to Barra, the Uists, Harris and Lewis. However, the legends associated with St Donan suggest that Eigg was outside the control of both kingdoms. The arrival of Christianity marks the end of the prehistoric period.

THE ARRIVAL OF THE SAINTS

Sunset: Poll Duchaill

With the coming of the monks from Iona to Eigg the island enters the era of written history. Christianity had first been re-established in Scotland by St Ninian, but its influence had been confined to Galloway. More important was the arrival in the Hebrides of the Irish monk, St Columba, bringing with him the traditions of the Celtic church.

This period in the seventh century represents the flowering of Celtic culture on both sides of the Irish sea, with Iona being recognised as a seat of learning in the Western Isles. In the history of the Celtic church, this period is known as the 'Age of the Saints'. The word 'saint' does not have exactly the meaning we associate with it today, but instead meant educated, or trained in a monastery. It was not only their learning, but also their evangelical zeal which made the Celtic saints so remarkable. After leaving Ireland with twelve disciples, St Columba founded his monastry on Iona in A.D. 563. It became the spiritual centre of Dalriada and also the base from which the conversion of pagan Pictland was undertaken. Almost all the Hebridean islands have traditions associated with a seventh-century saint but only St Donan was a martyr.

St Donan of Eigg was described as a friend of St Columba, and legend has it that St Columba visited Eigg, a hazardous journey of 40 miles by coracle from Iona. He is said to have charmed the snakes away from all the places he visited, and the lack of adders on Eigg has been used as proof of his visit there. He is commemorated in St Columba's well in Cleadale (the opposite side of the island from St Donan's monastery).

Despite a warning from St Columba that his venture would end in disaster, St Donan set up his monastery with 52 monks at Kildonnan. Tradition has it that his monastery was on the promontory overlooking the present harbour where a modern statue to the saint now stands. Here the archaeological remains are confused, but it seems that St Donan and his companions were reoccupying an Iron Age fort on the same site. Certainly, inside the fort there are slight traces of walls and possibly circular huts which may have been monastic buildings. If, however, his monastery was near the later and now ruined church and graveyard, then it has disappeared without trace. We can imagine the little community living in their stone huts roofed with turves on their rocky site commanding a view across to the mainland and over the harbour below.

We do not know how long St Donan and his monks remained unmolested 'in the place where the sheep of the queen of the country were kept' before they were attacked. It was long enough to gain the trust and friendship of the local inhabitants if one of the versions of the legend is to be believed. It says that the queen had to call in the aid of pirates to massacre the monks as the local people refused to do so. The martyrdom of St Donan is remembered in several island laments and the little ruined church was dedicated to him. Whether it was the queen or a piratical raid that was responsible for the murders, the monastery did not stay empty for long and Irish annals record an abbot of Eigg in 725 and 752. However, the monastery did not survive the Viking invasions.

By the eighth century the Celtic monasteries were accepting the traditions of Rome. Previously there had been no central organisation and each monastery was a self-governing unit with its own rules and order of mass. Gradually the Celtic church accepted the Roman method of calculating Easter and in 716 the monastery at Iona came under Roman obedience, although it was not until 1203 that it accepted the Benedictine Rule. The Celtic church which had kept Christianity alive in the western fringes of the British Isles and given the Gaelic culture an identity of its own now rejoined the mainstream of Christianity.

Although the principal religious site on the island was at Kildonnan, there were several crosses which probably marked preaching places. Their distribution, one at Grulin, one in Cleadale and one near Kildonnan church reflect the areas of population on the island. None of these crosses survive except as place-names, but they may well have been erected before the medieval period.

Our knowledge of the political control of Eigg in the eighth century, remains very hazy but we can guess at what life on the island was like. Its population would have lived in a few scattered settlements around the coast and in the small monastery overlooking the harbour. Here a few vessels, travelling up and down the coast and between the islands, might anchor to seek protection from a storm or to take on supplies. Although the monks may have travelled regularly to nearby monasteries, and on missionary ventures, there was little other contact with the outside world.

By the end of the eighth century, this situation had changed. The Vikings were raiding from Norway down the west coast of Scotland and probably made use of both the harbour below Kildonnan and Laig bay on the other side of the island for shelter. In 794 Skye was pillaged and wasted. In 797, 801, 823 and again in 985, Iona was plundered.

In the ninth century the Vikings began to settle and rule much of northern and western Scotland. Not until the Battle of Largs in 1263 was the power of the king of Norway in Scotland finally crushed, and for most of the period between 850 and 1263 the Hebrides were under Norse rule.

Like many who had come before them it was the areas around Laig bay (Lavik, or 'Surf bay' in Old Norse) and that overlooking the harbour below Kildonnan that the Vikings found most attractive and where remains have been found.

It is easy to imagine, when looking at the impressive curve of Laig bay how inviting this would have been to incoming settlers to beach their boats and come ashore. It is here, when drainage work was being carried out in the boggy land between Laig farm house and the sea, that just over 100 years ago two curved pieces of wood, each about two metres long, were found about ten metres apart, suggesting that they were the stem and stern post of a longboat. The finds, now in the Royal Museum of Scotland are unique in the British Isles, although similar posts have been found in Scandinavia. Tradition and topography suggest that the whole low-lying area behind the sand dunes was once a lake, and the discovery of these timbers lends support to this therory.

From the other side of the island, below Kildonnan farm, come the other Viking finds. In the Royal Museum of Scotland are the objects found in three burial mounds, one excavated in about 1830 and the others in 1875. Nothing remains of the earlier excavation site, but the circular stone hollows of the two graves excavated in 1875 can still be seen. The earlier excavation produced an ornate sword hilt, a hone, a silvered bronze brooch, part of a buckle and a cast-iron foot, probably from a large tripod cauldron. Finds from the 1875 excavations included pieces of woollen and linen material, a belt clasp, an iron axe head, some amber beads, a spindle whorl and part of a sickle. All these finds are fairly typical of a Viking grave dating from the mid-ninth century, but no traces of a body were found. The second smaller grave produced a bronze brooch, a hone, jet beads and part of an iron sword.

These finds need not indicate settlement, only that Eigg was a stopping place on the route around the west coast. However, the many

The bay of Laig

Viking place-names do suggest that Vikings did actually settle here in the period of their domination up to the 13th century. In 1098 a treaty acknowledging the Norwegian king's Lordship of the Isles was signed, but over the next 200 years he took little interest in the Western Isles, except to demand tribute, which was rather irregularly paid.

By the 12th century, the control of the Norwegian king was so weak that the Gaelic warrior, Somerled was able to expel the Norsemen from the west Highlands and establish himself as ruler of Argyll and some of the neighbouring islands. His son, Ranald is described as 'king of the Hebrides and Argyll' after Somerled's murder in 1164. Later, Eigg came under the control of another son, Angus, and then his nephew, Ruari. From the different branches of the Somerled family emerged the island clans.

The declining influence of Norway encouraged the Scottish crown to try and gain control of the Hebrides by attacking Skye and the Small Isles. The Macdonanlds and MacRuaris, preferring nominal Norwegian control to the potentially more effective Scottish rule, called for help against Alexander III from King Haakon

Above: Viking sword hilt found in a cairn at Kildonnan in 1878 and now in the Royal Museum of Scotland.

Below: One of the stem posts from a bog near Laig bay and very similar to ones found in Scandinavia. The reconstruction of a Viking boat shows the stem post in position.

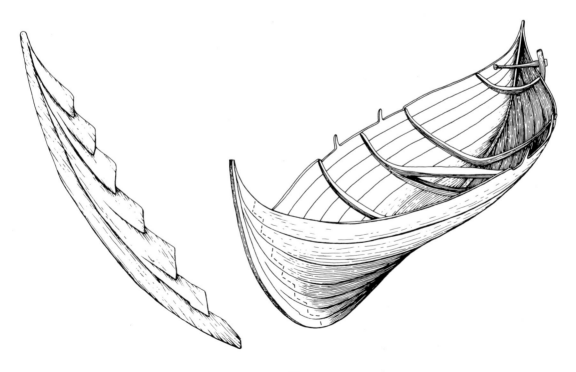

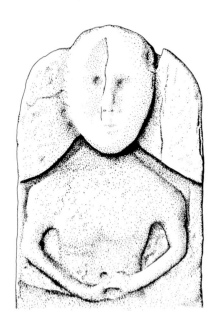

Primitive carving showing a figure apparently with exaggerated ears and previously kept in St Donan's church.

II of Norway. This last attempt to assert Norwegian control failed with the defeat of the Norwegian king at the Battle of Largs in 1263. The Western Isles then came, nominally at least, under the control of the king of Scotland. However, the island lords retained their lands and were mostly undisturbed by central authority. Eigg and Rhum were granted to the Macdonalds by Robert the Bruce in return for their support at Bannockburn in 1314. For this, the Macdonalds were expected to provide a ship of 26 oars with men and food. By 1354 John Macdonald was able to style himself 'Dominus Insularum' or Lord of the Isles. This period of virtual independence lasted for 144 years.

Much of Eigg's importance during this period lay in its convenient position between the mainland and island properties of the Macdonalds. Its location made it a suitable meeting place for the clan from the surrounding regions. For instance, when, John Macdonald died in 1386, his elder son, Ranald, already an old man, called a meeting of 'the gentlemen of the Isles, and his brothers' at Kildonnan. Ranald's younger brothers were sons of a second marriage to a daughter of Robert II and it had been arranged that the eldest of them, Donald, should inherit the Lordship of the Isles. At Kildonnan, therefore, Ranald gave the 'wand of Lordship' to Donald 'with the consent of his brethren and the nobles of the islands, all other persons being obedient to him'. Thus, Donald became the second Lord of the Isles. Ranald,

however, retained his mother's possessions, including Eigg and so was the founder of the Clanranalds who owned Eigg until 1828.

It was not until 1498 that the Scottish crown was strong enough to force the fourth Lord of the Isles to forfeit the Hebrides, but on two more occasions Eigg was the rallying point for rebellious lords. In 1543 a descendant of the Lord of the Isles fled to Eigg and met there the western chiefs who acknowledged his right to the title. From Eigg he sent commissioners to England to negotiate with Henry VIII against the Scottish crown, but although the rebels were paid by Henry, the revolt came to nothing.

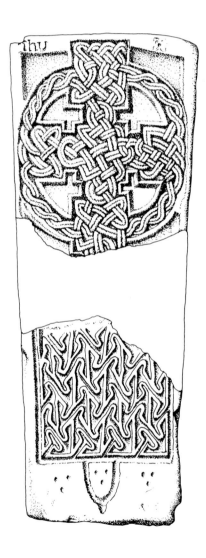

A cross slab of red sandstone, now in the porch of Eigg Lodge. The ringed cross head is decorated with typical Celtic interlace patterns while the key pattern on the shaft is more unusual.

Finally, when Sir James Macdonald, another descendant of the last Lord of the Isles escaped from Edinburgh Castle in 1615, he went to Eigg, where his supporters met him before invading Islay. That Eigg was already a valuable cattle rearing area is shown by the fact that, before departing, the rebels 'slaughtered a great supply of cattle to ensure themselves a good supply of provisions'. The invasion of Islay was a failure, but Sir James escaped into exile.

Above: Schist cross shaft decorated with leafy interlace pattern in the graveyard at Kildonnan, probably dating from the end of the 15th century. The cross head, although of similar design, is from a different cross.

FROM ANARCHY TO ORDER

Hoodie: Laig farm

The general lawlessness and lack of central control over these areas, remote and inaccessible from Edinburgh, shows that although the Scottish crown was able to break the islands' independence, it could not provide a stable alternative government. The 'massacre cave' episode is an example of the brutality typical of the period. The traditional story tells how, in 1577, a boat belonging to the Macleods was forced by bad weather to take refuge at Eigg. The Macleods of Harris claimed land on Skye occupied by the Macdonalds and so there was constant feuding. When the boat crew asked for food and shelter, they were refused and set adrift. Some versions of the story claim that the behaviour of the boat crew on landing justified this unfeeling treatment. In revenge, the Macleods returned from Harris burning houses and crops. The frightened inhabitants took shelter in a cave and the only person the Macleods could find was an old lady whom they spared, but as they were sailing away they caught sight of a scout sent out from the cave and following his tracks back, they found the hiding place, lit a fire in the mouth of the cave and so suffocated the 398 island inhabitants.

There are many caves around the rocky coast of Eigg, but the one associated with this story is called Uamh Fhraing, south-west of the pier (NM475834) and easily approached by a path from Galmisdale. The entrance is long and narrow, but inside, the tunnel widens out into quite a large cavern in which possibly 400 people could have sheltered. The full story had been written down by 1680 and the brave words of the lone old woman were recorded. When told that she would not be killed, but that all the food would be taken from the island, she said, 'If I get the shell fish of Sloc, the dulse of Lag '(Laig) 'and the tender water cress, and drink from the well at Tolain, I shall not want.' Later the story was told to James Boswell in 1773 when there were said to be skeletons in the cave. Sir Walter Scott saw bones in 1814 and even took a souvenir home with him. In 1845, Sir Hugh Miller, touring the Hebrides in 'The Betsey', described in detail the piles of bones, lying as if in family groups and still to be seen in the cave. Soon after they were collected and buried, but surprisingly, no one recorded where. A child's skull was found in the cave in the 1970s but this has not been dated.

The island was soon afterwards reoccupied from the surrounding area, but there was yet another massacre in 1588 when the whole population was killed by Lachlen Maclean of Duart and his men. The register of the Privy Council recorded that, 'The like barbarous and shameful cruelty has seldom been seen among Christians in any kingdom or age.' Five years later, in a description of the island compiled for James VI, James Stewart of Appin provides the earliest evidence for the cave story when he describes the caverns around the coast and says briefly that the Macleods 'smorit the haill people thairin to the number of 395 personnes, men, wyfe and bairnis.' He went on to describe the island as pertaining to the Clanranalds and to be valued as '30 mark land'. By 1593 it had recovered from the massacres enough to raise 60 men for war.

There is no doubt that at this date the danger of the island population being wiped out either by massacre or famine was very real. Before the introduction of the potato, the main crop had been oats with a little barley for brewing. During the second half of the 16th century, 24 years out of 50 were marked by high food prices in the Highlands, a sure sign of scarcity. There were many years in the 1570s and '90s when people died of starvation. Although there was a general improvement in the 17th century, the famine years of 1695-9 were the worst for a 100 years. It was at such times that the islanders would have resorted to the practice of bleeding their animals for blood to mix with their oats in an effort to eke their food out a bit further. In the event of a total population being wiped out it would be in the chieftain's interest to repopulate by moving people in rather than leave the island open to attack and this must be the explanation for the apparent rapid recovery of population after the massacres and famines.

The fact that the population was totally wiped out at least once in the 17th century is shown by the lack of early oral tradition on the island, which does not go back as far as that found on other islands. The Rev. Swanson, protestant minister in the 1830s and early '40s, believed that none of the island families pre-dated the massacre. 'Most of the present inhabitants can tell which of their ancestors, grandfathers or great grandfathers first settled in the place and where they came from; and with the exception of a few vague legends about St Donan and his grave, which were preserved, apparently among the people of the other Small Isles, the island has no traditional history.

Landholding in these years of civil disorder was organised on a military basis. The Clanranalds installed chief tenants or 'tacksmen' who were frequently relatives of the family, one at

Kildonnan and often one at Laig as well. They were not usually concerned with farming, and their main responsibility was to make sure that the 60 men mentioned in the 1593 'Description of the Isles of Scotland' were available if needed. In order to provide this number of fighting men, the population had to be kept as high as possible and these people would be maintained on the island's communal townships where land was farmed in common and all shared in the paying of rent.

It was during the anarchic years of the 16th century that the present church at St Donan is said to have been erected by John Moydartach, Captain of Clanranald. There is some evidence for an earlier church on the site. Casts of four medieval crosses are now in the porch of Eigg Lodge while the originals are in the Royal Museum of Scotland. One 15th-century cross shaft still stands in the church yard with the head of a different cross beside it. An older and more primitive carving also associated with the site depicts a human head and shoulders and is a further indication that there must have been a church on the site from the early post-Viking period.

The present building is a very simple one of massive stone walls with one door in the south wall and only two very small windows in the east end, all typical of building construction at the time. The church is now roofless and inside it is very overgrown, but there are two grave slabs with incised crosses on the floor and a tomb recessed into the north wall at the east end. Although it is now very difficult to see the sculptured heraldic symbols on it, in the 1870s they were much clearer and were identified as emblems of the Clanranalds with a date of 1641. The tomb is said to contain the bones of Raghall MacAileen Oig (Ronald MacDonald), a member of the Morar branch of the Clanranalds who held land at Arisaig as well as the farm at Sandavore on Eigg. He was a great piper who both composed and taught and was the author of some of the most famous pipe music still played, including the Glas Mheur. It was his funeral cortege that halted on the road from Grulin to await the chief mourner from Arisaig.

The Reformation in Scotland took place in 1560 when the Calvinist teachings of John Knox became the official religion. After 1560 the Roman Catholic church was illegal and the celebration of mass was punishable by death. Priests were banished, but in remote areas there were no pastors to replace them. It was not until the 1620s that a Protestant minister was appointed to the Small Isles. It must have been at that time that the church at Kildonnan fell derelict, and it was another 280 years before a new Church of Scotland church was built. Much of Eigg, along with most of north-west Scotland remained Catholic, and this was yet another

The tomb of Raghall Mac Aileen Oig (Ronald MacDonald), in the chapel at Kildonnan drawn in 1878, when the heraldic emblems were clearer than they are today.

factor that set this area outside the effective control of the crown. Secret Roman Catholic missionaries from Gaelic colleges in Spain were active in the Highlands in the early 17th century and there were nearly 200 'converts' on Eigg. It was not so much that the people had previously been Protestants; rather they had received no religious instruction since the 1560s. Wherever the priests went, they were shocked by the lack of religious knowledge amongst the people. Eigg became a refuge for Catholics from the neighbouring islands. When the Protestant owner of Rhum, Maclean of Coll, insisted in the 1720s, that the inhabitants gave up their Catholicism, some moved to Eigg and Clanranald found them land.

It was not only religion, but also language that kept the Highlands and Islands apart from the rest of Scotland. Gaelic was still spoken throughout the region and the division between Gaelic, Catholic areas and the English speaking, Protestant ones was brought to the fore when James II of England and VII of Scotland lost his throne to Mary, daughter of James I and VI and her Protestant Dutch husband, William. The Catholic clans remained loyal to the Stewarts in exile. The result was the massacre of the MacDonalds of Glencoe and a period of repression throughout the Highlands, including attempts to stamp out the Gaelic language. An act of 1696 allowed for the setting up of schools teaching the Protestant faith in English, and by 1698 there were 25 such schools on permanent sites in Gaelic Scotland, while 13 more were peripatetic. In 1709, the Scottish Society for the Propagation of Christian Knowledge was founded to set up schools where none as yet existed. From 1725 the Society received a government grant of £1,000 a year towards its work in the hope that it would help break support for the Jacobite cause. In 1728 a schoolmaster was sent to Eigg and Canna. At that time there were 340 people over the age of five on Eigg, but few of them showed much enthusiasm for the sectarian education offered, and in 1811 there was still no permanent school on the island. This suspicion was not so much of education in general but of English Protestant education in particular as is shown by the interest in the schools set up by the Gaelic School Society after 1812. One was established on Eigg by the fundamentalist minister, the Rev. Swanson shortly before his eviction at the time of the Disruption which separated the Free and Established Church of Scotland in 1843-4.

By the early 18th century the years of the arbitary power of the clan chieftains were coming to an end. The grand courts such as that of Sir Roy Macleod of Dunvegan a hundred years previously were a thing of the past. Here he had entertained lavishly and supported relatives, pipers, fiddlers and poets. The establishment was kept up by the payments in kind from his tenants. Skye alone provided him with 400 stone of butter a year.

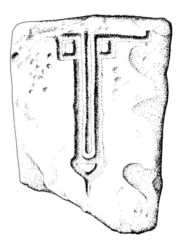

Part of a cross, now in the porch of Eigg lodge.

In 1609, the island chiefs had been forced to sign the Statutes of Iona by the bishop, representing the government. Amongst the terms which the highland lords had to agree to was the rebuilding of ruined churches, which involved the acceptance of alien Calvinist traditions and the limiting of the size of households kept by chieftains. Bards, who had been the bearers of Gaelic culture and were therefore regarded as subversive, as well as beggars and vagabonds were not to be received on the islands. Of great importance was the ruling that any chieftain or yeoman worth in goods 60 cows or more must send his eldest son to the lowlands to be educated in English.

In 1703, Martin Martin, writing of the Western Isles said that it was 60 years since a new chieftain had been put to the test by making him lead a raid on his neighbours before he was accepted. Gradually the ways of the south were assimilated, even before Culloden. Law and order was beginning to improve, and market forces were penetrating the Highlands as more cattle were taken south for sale. Highland lords were travelling and taking on the values of the more sophisticated and opulent aristocracies of France and England.

THE END OF THE CLANRANALDS

Storm delivered kelp

The final test of the clan system came at the Battle of Culloden in 1745 with the last of the Jacobite rebellions against the house of Hanover. Much of the support for Charles Stewart was to be found in the north-west of Scotland, although some of it was given rather reluctantly. Many of the tacksmen and their followers in Lochaber, for instance, were unenthusiastic supporters of the cause. Support in Roman Catholic areas was strongest, so it is not surprising that men from Eigg were found fighting with the young Clanrananld beside Charles Stewart under John Macdonald of Laig. After the defeat at Culloden, some of Clanranald's followers fled to Eigg where 38 were picked up by the British navy in May 1746. Thirty six were tried, sentenced and transported to Barbados where they died. Charles Stewart even considered setting up his headquarters on Eigg early in 1746 and this may be why the island was visited twice by Royal Navy vessels. However, in September Charles finally left the Highlands for France and the rising was over.

Changes in the Scottish way of life which had begun with the Act of Union with England in 1707 were accelerated after the Jacobite rebellion. Glasgow merchants who from 1707 were allowed unrestricted access to England's commercial empire, pioneered industrial change in and around Glasgow. Interest in agricultural progress also increased and the lowlands of Scotland soon came to rank with the progressive areas of East Anglia as an area of intensive cereal production. The contrast between this and the archaic systems of the Highlands became very obvious, particularly to the increasing number of clan chiefs who now travelled to Edinburgh, London and Paris. Change was also encouraged by the agricultural improvers, constantly seeking new lands to develop.

It was the policy of the British government after Culloden to break the clan system. The semi-independent rule of the chieftains was becoming an anachronism in a state trying to enforce central control, and they were encouraged to go south. The period of Edinburgh's cultural and academic achievement began.

To participate in this life of high society, the lairds needed money as never before and this created new problems. They ceased to be the respected heads of their clans and instead became absentee landlords hoping to be able to afford a life of fashion and leisure on an income generated on remote highland estates. However, the existing system of landholding based on military service could not produce the necessary money, and so attempts were made to reorganise the whole basis of landholding in the Highlands. Travel opened the chieftains' eyes to the great changes that were taking place in the south which they now wanted to extend to the north. The final end of the chief as a military leader whose prestige was based on the number of soldiers he could raise came after Culloden. Social standing then came to be measured in terms of income and conspicuous consumption. Boswell observed in 1773 that 'The system of things is now so much altered that the family cannot have influence, except by riches.' To increase his income it was therefore necessary for the highland landlord to break up the old communal farms which allowed a large population of potential clan warriors to live off a small area of land, and replace them with tenanted farms of a southern type; a system which supported fewer people but commanded higher rents when converted to cattle or sheep production.

The increasing population in the south meant that there was a great demand, firstly for cattle and later for sheep, and so prices went up. Sheep farming had reached the southern uplands of Scotland by 1720, but until 1770 cattle farming for the southern market was more important. After 1770 the price of sheep and wool began to increase with rises particularly dramatic in the Revolutionary Wars against France (1796-1815). As prices increased, so did the rent for land. A large farm on Skye that was let for £16 per annum early in the century was let for £50 in 1772. The possibility of raising rents by two or three fold was a great incentive to the Scottish landlords to follow the example of those further south. The problem was that this involved breaking up a type of communal peasant farming that had long disappeared in the south. The new commercial farms would support a far smaller population than the old subsistence ones and many landlords saw emigration as the obvious way of getting rid of the surplus population. Boswell and Johnson found that this was a frequent topic of conversation when they toured the Hebrides in 1773. However, the importance of the area for the recruiting of men for the prestigious highland regiments meant that official government policy was likely to be against emigration.

Shortly after this date another source of wealth for the landlords of the coastal estates became apparent. This was the harvesting and drying of kelp to produce soda ash, valuable in the manufacture of soap, glass and particularly, gunpowder. This needed a large workforce so rather than encouraging people to leave, landlords forcibly resettled the inhabitants on smallholdings, or 'crofts', along the coast. As the work with the kelp was seasonal, it was necessary for the workforce to have some other means of livelihood and this was provided on the smallholding.

When the communal farms were broken up, the obvious people to take over the new farms were the tacksmen. However, they regarded this as a lowering of their social position and many left, often for America, leaving a large gap in the social order. This gap was filled by outsiders from the south who were experienced sheep farmers, looking for new and possibly cheaper rented land.

Even without the problems of land reorganisation, life for the small tenants was far from easy; Boswell and Johnson were very well aware of the poverty around them on their travels. Crops failed, often as frequently as one year in three, and an observer wrote in 1794, 'The hardships of the peasants appear to arise merely from the disadvantages of the local situation rather than any systematic oppression of the landlords.' In 1776 the inhabitants of Rhum were described as 'a well-made and well looking race, but carry famine in their aspect.' They raised good crops of potatoes but 'so small a quantity of barley and oats that there is not a quarter produced to supply their annual wants: all the subsistence the poor people have besides, is curds, milk and fish.' Rhum was an island well known for the paternalism of its landlord who certainly could have made more profit by letting it as a few larger farms.

In 1811 it was said that 'Mr Maclean of Coll might let as a sheep walk his large island of Rhum containing upwards of 20,000 Scotch ewes at a profit of several hundred pounds per annum to two or three farmers instead of the present 350 inhabitants who possess it for a mere trifle, could he find any means of providing for the poor people consistent with his patriotism and humanity'. A later land owner was not to have the same scruples when he cleared a large part of the island in 1826.

The survival of such relatively large populations in such inhospitable terrain was entirely the result of the introduction of the potato, said to have been planted for the first time in the Hebrides in 1743 by Macdonald of Clanranald on his return from a visit to relatives in Ireland. It very quickly increased in

Meg at Laig

popularity until by 1811 it provided four fifths of the human food and a third of the animal fodder consumed on the islands. The cultivation of the potato enabled the large populations that the landlords needed to work in the kelp harvest to be maintained on small plots whilst the rest of the agricultural land could be let as large stock farms.

As early as 1788 the process of reorganising the farms on Eigg had begun. Laig and Kildonnan farms were already worked as single units by tacksmen outside the communal system. Ronald Macdonald came to Eigg and took over Laig farm and the neighbouring townships. When his daughter, Mary, married, he evicted tenants from Cleadale to create a farm for the couple, and he built them a house near where the Roman Catholic chapel now stands. The tenants from this Cleadale township were amongst the first from Eigg to emigrate to America. Mary's husband refused to live in the new farm because of the evictions that had made its creation possible. All the family later died in either mysterious or tragic circumstances, due, as legend has it, to the curses of the evicted tenants.

The Clanranald family were in great financial difficulties by the end of the 18th century. They were part of the extravagent fashionable circle that surrounded the Prince Regent, and their lifestyle was far outside that which could be supported by their poor highland estates. Attempts had to be made to improve the income from these possessions and the decision was made to reorganise Eigg into tenant farms and small crofts to which the inhabitants of the townships would be moved, thus forcing them to concentrate on the production of the very valuable kelp in order to earn a living. It was generally agreed that this would be a more efficient and therefore profitable system, the old run-rig farming based on townships being regarded as a 'careless and outdated mode.' It was not to be expected that the newly created farms would be taken on by any of the local population who had a 'superstitious reverence for old practices and an undiscriminating abhorrence of innovation.' Instead they would be let to stock farmers, often from the lowlands who had the capital and knowledge to run intensive sheep or cattle enterprises.

There certainly was a need for some changes to be made on the island. Although it was described as being 'fertile and well cultivated' in the late 18th century, the population was growing fast, from about 450 in the 1760s, to 500 by the end of the century, and most

Island Cheviots at Grulin

observers felt that a reduction of population was needed. However, emigration was not likely to be encouraged by the Clanranalds whilst there was kelp to be worked.

Despite the growth of kelp production, the records for the years 1801-1811 show the greatest decrease in population in the first half of the 19th century: from 500 to 442. The most likely cause of this was the intensified recruitment by the navy and the highland regiments. Press gangs were active on Eigg and several islanders served under Wellington in the Peninsular War. One widow from Brae, above Kildonnan lost all her four sons, one by one, to the press gang. Although the loss of her three eldest was sad enough, it was when her youngest son, Hector, was taken that she was moved to compose a lament expressing her grief. If only her youngest had been spared, she sang, then she could have borne the loss of the three older ones. A few verses of this song are still remembered on the island today.

Before any changes could be made, an accurate map of the island, showing exact acreages of cultivated land and common pasture was needed and this was drawn by William Bald in 1806. William Bald was a highly skilled surveyor who later became an eminent engineer. His large-scale map of Eigg, like several others he drew in north-west Scotland, the islands and Ireland, was drawn to a very high standard for the day. It shows each individual building, (although it is not clear which are dwellings and which are outbuildings) as well as the confused pattern of the run-rig cultivation strips in the open fields, frequently interrupted by outcrops of rock, areas of scree and marsh. They had not been laid out at one time, but expanded gradually over the centuries as the needs of the population required. The stone walls of these nebulous patches can be seen at Grulin and underlying the straight croft boundaries all over Cleadale and to the north of Howlin.

The map confirms that by the early 19th century the island was densely populated with every available bit of land cultivated. There were over 100 buildings, (in 1831 there were 74 inhabited houses) and over 1,000 acres of cultivated land. Another 1,000 acres was pasture while 3,500 were high moor. The map shows Eigg divided into ten townships, each consisting of a scattered group of between seven and 15 buildings surrounded by strips all hand-dug and only those nearest the houses would have been

TOWNSHIPS ON THE ISLE OF EIGG, 1806
(from William Bald's map)

TOWNSHIP	ACREAGE OF ARABLE	ACREAGE OF PASTURE	ACREAGE OF LOCHS	ACREAGE OF MOOR
Upper Grulin	59	16	6	402
Lower Grulin	54	3	14	601
Galmisdale	128	42		407
Sandavore	69	23		165
Sandaveg	23			359
Glebe 78	27			
Kildonnan	197	369		406
Laig	79	?c.100		806
Cleadale	194	209		397
Five Pennies	66	103		
Howlin	67	200		102
TOTAL	1013	1002	20	3649

William Bald's map of 1806 measures about 1.5 X 1.2 metres and hangs in the hall of Eigg Lodge. It was drawn for the Clanranalds in 1806 when an accurate survey of the island was needed in advance of the reorganisation of the communal farms into crofts and shows the cultivated area as shown on Bald's map (just over 1,000 acres). Every available bit of flat land was ploughed up, even Castle Island. Some of the township boundaries can still be followed across the moors as dry-stone dykes. The table of acreages is also from the map and gives the amount of arable, pasture and moorland within each parish.

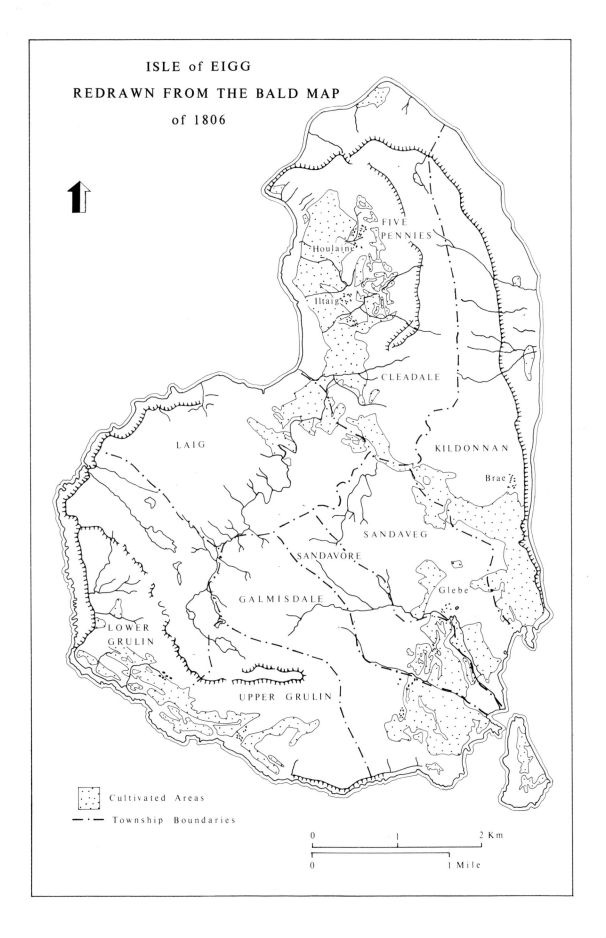

ISLE of EIGG
REDRAWN FROM THE BALD MAP
of 1806

FIVE
PENNIES

Houlaine

Iltaig

CLEADALE

LAIG

KILDONNAN

Brae

SANDAVEG

SANDAVORE

Glebe

GALMISDALE

LOWER
GRULIN

UPPER GRULIN

Cultivated Areas

Township Boundaries

0   1   2 Km

0   1 Mile

Kildonnan mill

cultivated every year. The others would revert to pasture for several years between each crop. The rows of these 'lazy beds', or run-rig strips, each about 1.5 metres wide can still be seen all over the island, particularly when the evening or early morning sun casts long shadows. They are even perched high up on hillsides, wherever there is a small area of flat land, and are a reminder of the acute land shortage and population pressures of the early 19th century. A close comparison between a recent aerial photograph showing the surviving run-rig system as indicated by the earth-works and the lines of run-rig shown on Bald's map do show significant differences of direction. It appears, therefore, that while Bald was showing areas of cultivation accurately, his depiction of the details of layout may have been somewhat arbitrary.

There is little to distinguish one settlement from the next. Only Kildonnan, consisting of a single farm and a mill, is different; it was farmed by the minister's son, Donald Macaskill, who, although a doctor, chose to farm. He was the most substantial farmer on the island, with 197 acres of arable and 369 of pasture. He was also the estate representative in charge of the allocation of crofts in Cleadale when the reorganisation took place in 1810.

An Sgurr and Galmisdale house, once an estate farm

Sheep fank at Sandavore

We know very little about this major event in the island's history when families were moved lock, stock and barrel to their new homes. For instance, none of the houses shown on the Bald map in Cleadale survived the reorganisation. In contrast, the Grulin townships were not reorganised, which may explain why they were so vulnerable to clearance later.

The results of these changes can be seen both in the present-day landscape and in the enumerator's lists for the 1841 census. On the south-west of the island, the townships of Upper and Lower Grulin and Galmisdale, and in the north-west, Cleadale, became crofting areas, with almost all the heads of households described as 'crofters' in 1841. Cleadale was particularly involved in the exploitation of kelp. In 1811 'Considerable quantities of kelp are made on Eigg, especially on the western side where there is a beautiful semi-amphitheatre fenced with a natural enclosure of rocks adapted to the cultivation of corn and the manufacture of kelp.'

When the crofts were first laid out they were only intended to provide part of the income of the crofters. The price of kelp had risen dramatically during the Napoleonic Wars. Between 1808 and 1810 Reginald Macdonald of Clanranald made the enormous sum of £42,000 from the kelp produced on Eigg and Canna. About 15,000 to 20,000 tons of kelp ash was exported annually from the Hebrides as a whole at this time. The pattern of farming changed to allow as much time as possible for the summer kelp harvest. Potatoes could be produced with less effort during the summer months than cereals and so they increased in importance at the expense of oats. Kelping certainly provided much needed secondary employment, but took from the land the attention it really needed. Reliance on the potato meant that the necessity for crop rotations was ignored. Seaweed, which had been valued as a fertiliser could no longer be spared for the land.

Kelping itself was a thoroughly unpleasant task involving spending long hours in the very cold water collecting the seaweed and then carting it, usually in creels carried on the back, to areas where it could dry before being burnt in the kilns. Sometimes horses were used, but if so, they needed feeding and pasturing, thus taking scarce land. Visitors from the south, steeped in the values of a newly industrialised Britain where the virtues of hard disciplined work were encouraged, were heartened to see the Hebrideans transformed from 'idle loiterers in a state of comparative uselessness into excellent workmen and persevering steady labourers.'

With the end of the Napoleonic Wars, however, the market for kelp collapsed, leaving a heavily populated island with no means of support, except the crofts. The population continued to rise and every available piece of ground was hand-dug for potatoes. Seaweed or other manure was laid in a strip on the ground and then the earth on either side was piled up on it. As the population rose, land could not be allowed to rest fallow and as a result, fertility and yields declined. The only solution to the problem created by the end of the kelp boom seemed to be mass emigration. An official report of 1837 stated, 'It must be admitted that few cases could arise to which the remedy of emigration on a large scale would appear more appropriate than that of the Hebrides.' In 1826, 300 people were shipped from Rhum and the island let as a single sheep farm. As a result the rent rose from £300 to £800. Landlords had previously valued the crofter population, which they themselves had created, for kelping. Now it was simply a nuisance.

After the failure of kelp, the only source of profit for the landlords was their large farms, but this was not enough to save the Clanranalds. By 1827 Reginald Macdonald, 20th Captain of Clanranald, had worked his way through the family fortune and so after more than four centuries the estate was sold. Eigg was bought by Dr Hugh MacPherson, whose family owned it until the 1890s. Unlike the previous owners, the MacPhersons spent much of their time on the island, converting a pair of cottages near the harbour into a home and taking an interest in island affairs and particularly its antiquities.

A CENTURY OF CHANGE

Cleadale: House ruin, haycock and croft boundary dykes

1841 was the year for which the census recorded the highest population on Eigg as 546, and the schoolmaster wrote on the census form that this was more than the island could really support. 'There is a small increase in the population of this island since 1831 which I consider to have been on account of more marriages having taken place in the last few years than has usually been the case. There is an abundant population on the island at present; consequently, when there is a failure of their small crops which is too often the case, especially of late years, the poor are doomed to suffer much privation and destitution. They would gladly follow their friends to Her Majesty's colonies in North America where a great many of the inhabitants of the Small Isles have emigrated several years ago, but in their present circumstances I do not think that most of them are even able to pay their passage across the Atlantic.' The schoolmaster added that there had been 'no emigration from the island in the previous six years.'

In 1845, Hugh Miller noticed the great poverty of many on the island. He met 'an old worn out man (whose wife had been bedridden for 10 years) with famine written legibly in his hollow cheek and eye.' They had no means of living except through the charity of their poor neighbours who had little enough to spare, 'and this is but one of many examples which the island of Eigg will be found to furnish.' In Cleadale every available piece of land was planted with cereals. 'The cottages lie in groups and, save where bogs . . . interpose their shag of dark green and break the continuity, the plain around them waves with corn, lying fair, green and populous within the sweep of its inaccessible rampart of rock.'

Alongside the overcrowded crofts were the tenanted farms of Laig, Sandavore and Kildonnan. By 1841 Laig, which had 13 houses in 1806, consisted only of three cottages and one farm house large enough to accommodate eight living-in servants (probably both farmworkers and domestic servants). Other than this the settlement consisted of two agricultural labourers, one shepherd and a clergyman.

Kildonnan had always been little more than a farm and a mill. The occupier of the house, Hugh Macdonald, was described as a tacksman in 1841. He housed 14 servants, and a 'charity boy' also lived with him. The land of Kildonnan farm stretched right up the east coast of the island and in a very remote and beautiful position on a fertile terrace between the high cliffs of the moor and the sea cliffs below are the ruins of a shieling (NM496889). It was occupied in the summer by two or three dairy maids from Kildonnan farm who spent their time making butter and cheese from the milk produced on the surrounding lush pasture. Hugh Miller passed this way in 1845 and wrote, 'Rarely have I seen a more interesting spot or one that, from utter loneliness so impressed the imagination.' He has also left us with a description of the shieling which gives much detail, especially about the interior of the dwelling. There was a pond in front, fed by the stream which still cascades over the cliff above, 'where a few milch cows were leisurely slaking their thirst'. Inside the house 'there was a turf fire at one end at which sat two little girls keeping the blaze under a large pot..the other end was occupied by a bed of dry straw spread on the floor from wall to wall and fenced off at the foot by a wall of stones. The middle space was occupied by the utensils and produce of the dairy, flat wooden vessels of milk, a butter churn and a tub half filled with curd while a few cheeses, soft from the press, lay on a shelf above.' He was struck by the solitary life of the three girls living there. 'They must often feel lonely when night has closed darkly over the mountain and sea and on those dreary days of mist and rain so common in the Hebrides when nought may be seen save the few shapeless crags that stud the nearer hillocks around there and nought heard save the moaning of the wind in the precipice above or the measured dash of the waves on the wild beach below.'

Sandavore appears to have been a communal farm in 1806, but in 1818 was taken over by the island's minister who farmed it alongside his glebe and Castle Island. In 1841 it was let to Allan MacKinnon who farmed 60 acres. The rest of the inhabitants of the township were agricultural labourers, farm servants, stockmen and a shepherd. As well as these there were two teachers, one of them Gaelic speaking, the minister and a merchant.

Very soon after 1841, the island's population began to decline and some settlements were deserted. In 1841 there were 89 inhabited houses, but by 1861 only 55. Much of this depopulation was voluntary rather than the result of planned clearances. Such a desertion was that at the settlement near the shepherd's house at Howlin, known as Five Pennies (NM476900). A penny-land was a land unit based on taxation in Norse times; it was equivalent to about eight acres and was valued as being able to support eight cows and two horses. In 1841 and 1851 there were seven inhabited houses, but by 1861 only Howlin and two houses remained in use. The stone walls of 16 buildings can still be seen exactly as they appear on William Bald's map. There is also the remains of a lime kiln. The burning and application of lime to help fertilise the acid soil was a very important part of agricultural practice on Eigg.

It is significant that all the inhabitants of Five Pennies were described as either agricultural labourers or cottars who had no right to any land, and so they were probably more ready to move than the crofters close by in Cleadale as they had little to lose. They would also have been some of the poorest inhabitants of the island unable to afford the passage to America: instead they would have gone to the industrial south.

There had been many changes before 1851, but there were to be more still in the following years. Like Five Pennies, the small township of Brae had contained no crofters. There were 11 houses in 1806, but only seven in 1841 and these were occupied by agricultural labourers, a shepherd, and a 'poor cottager.' The stockman, Hugh MacKinnon, had worked for Macdonald on his farm on South Uist. He was originally from Coll and had decided to emigrate to America. However, off Ireland the boat was found to be unsafe and so he worked his way, first to South Uist and then to Eigg.

Shortly after 1851, the last inhabitants left Brae, and the Kildonnan farmer constructed sheep folds there. The remains of some of the Brae houses can still be seen (NM492865) but

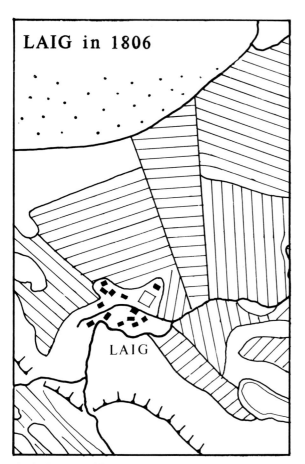

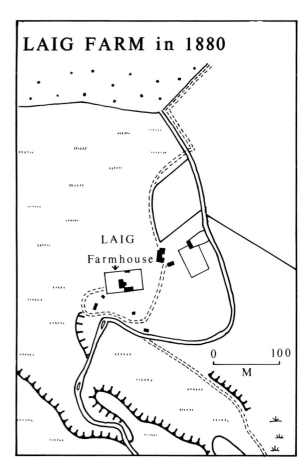

Left: Laig in 1806 showing buildings and cultivated strips. The township of Laig included fields on the fertile soils surrounding Laig bay, much of which was later included in the new croft land for the settlement at Chuagach.

Right: Laig farm in 1880. There is very little sign of the 13 buildings marked beside the bend in the burn in 1806. Other than the farm house and outbuildings, there is a possible house site beside the burn near the substantial footings for a bridge (NM463876). At some time between 1806 and 1880 an attempt was made to improve the drainage of the low-lying fields by cutting a deep channel for the burn and it now runs from the farm directly northwards to the sea.

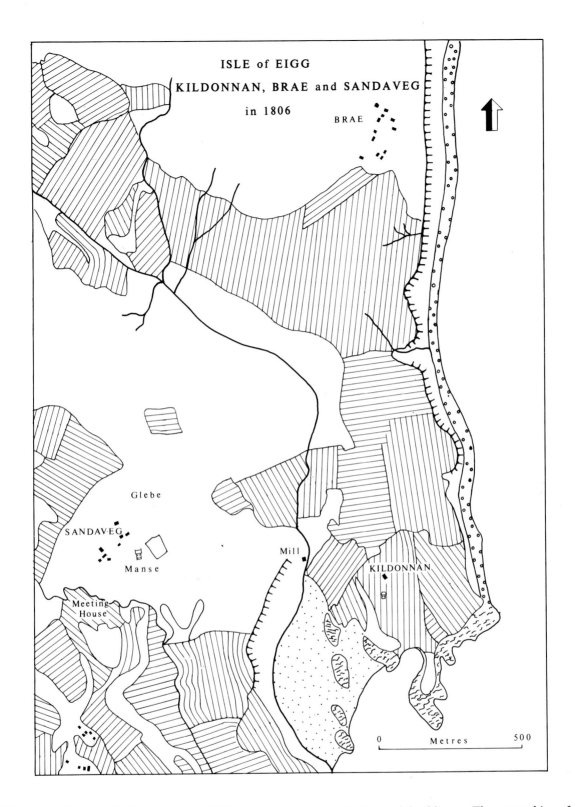

ISLE of EIGG

KILDONNAN, BRAE and SANDAVEG

in 1806

BRAE

Glebe

SANDAVEG

Manse

Meeting House

Mill

KILDONNAN

0   Metres   500

Kildonnan, Brae and Sandaveg in 1806, showing run-rig fields and buildings. The township of Kildonnan consisted only of a farm house, mill and chapel but there was still a sizeable settlement of 13 houses at Brae and eight at Sandaveg to the west of the manse. The manse is drawn in elevation on the map and certainly the ruins that remain today suggest that it was a very substantial building (NM484853).

fewer are preserved than elsewhere, presumably because the stones from the houses were used to build the very substantial sheep folds still standing on the site.

The late 1840s were horrific years in the Highlands and Islands because of the disastrous failures of the potato crops upon which the population relied. Between 1847 and 1857 about 16,000 people left north-west Scotland for the U.S.A., Canada, Australia and New Zealand. Many thousands more went south into the lowlands. The land they left was not, however, divided amongst the remaining crofters, but added to the large farms, so that the land starvation of the smallholder was not helped by their leaving.

To begin with Eigg escaped the potato blight, and Macfarlane who had the tack of Kildonnan from Hugh Macdonald was able to make great profits shipping potatoes from Eigg to the stricken areas. He even built his own pier, still known as Macfarlane's Pier for his potato boats. Throughout much of the mainland there was a very real danger of famine. Various relief agencies were set up under a Central Board of Management and their immediate and remarkable achievement was to prevent mass starvation. However, relief was only given in return for labour performed, usually on public works. On the mainland Mallaig harbour was constructed, and on Eigg the farmer at Laig, Angus Macdonald, was asked whether he would consider a government-sponsored drainage scheme to provide employment. He was much disheartened by the prevailing conditions and replied that he was thinking of emigrating, but that if he stayed he might drain. His three uncles had gone abroad, to India and Australia, and so the tradition of seeking a living across the seas was strong amongst the Macdonalds as in many other island families. In 1853, at the age of 24, he went to Wisconsin in Canada and the farm fell vacant. The last of the Clanranald tacksmen had finally left the island.

Although it is quite possible that the desertions at Five Pennies and Brae were voluntary, those from the Grulins were not; the agony of their clearance is still very much part of the folk memory of Eigg. When Laig farm was relet, the only potential taker was a border sheep farmer, Stephen Stewart, who was only interested if he could clear Upper and Lower Grulin and have these good grazing lands as well. It was the farmers from the south who saw the potential of a farm such as Laig for sheep.

The population of the Grulins had certainly been declining before the clearance, but unlike the people at Five Pennies and Brae, they were mostly crofters. In 1841 there had been 20 houses in the two settlements with a total of 103 inhabitants. Ten years later there were only 57 people left, all of whom, except for one family that remained as shepherds, were forcibly removed in 1853. Another family was able to take on a croft at Cleadale, but the rest were shipped to Nova Scotia to start a new life there. It was said that the pasture at the Grulins was so good that for the first years all the ewes produced twins. This sloping area of green hospitable land lying between the steep cliffs of An Sgurr and the sea still has some of the best grass on the island. However, Stewart's farming venture cannot have been a great success as he did not stay very long. Laig was then let to Roderick MacRae from Ross-shire, who remained until the 1880s.

The clearance of Grulin brought to an end a settlement that may have been continuous since Prehistoric times, as suggested by the prehistoric structures already mentioned on the hill behind. A medieval cross site to the south-east of Upper Grulin shows that the area was occupied in the Middle Ages, and the great number and variety of house sites shows that it must have been occupied over a long period. Most of the houses were round-cornered 'black houses' of a type found throughout the Highlands well into the 20th century. They would have had hipped roofs covered with peat and the four corner stones immediatly below the roof line projected out to support the hip rafters. Some house walls still stand to this level, a height of not more than one and a half metres. The houses did not usually have windows, most of the light coming through a central doorway. One house had bread ovens in one corner and some had animal enclosures or gardens beside them. There is one lime kiln for preparing local stone for use as a fertiliser, a practice that continued well into living memory. It is unlikely that all the houses that can be seen amongst the boulders and bracken were occupied at one time. A new generation would have built new houses and the old ones would have become sheds and outhouses.

The first settlement the visitor reaches when following the track from Galmisdale is Upper Grulin, where, by 1806 the houses were concentrated along both sides of a small stream which crosses the path (NM455852). Eleven houses are shown on the 1806 map and ten were occupied in 1841, but the ruins of more than 30 buildings can still be seen scattered over an extensive area.

Pony at Howlin

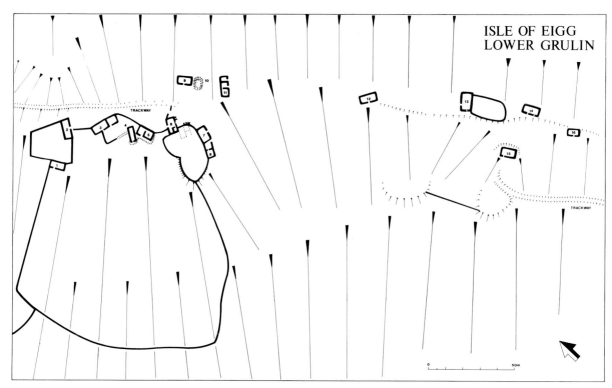

The 1986 survey of Lower Grulin. This was always a far smaller settlement than Upper Grulin. Buildings 1 to 8 may have made up one substantial holding.

Houses 1 to 15, Upper Grulin, and Muck

Lower Grulin is just half a mile further west and is spread out along both sides of the path (NM447851); in 1806 it consisted of nine houses, but ruins of nearly twice that number remain. Below the path are stone-walled enclosures which must be old field boundaries. This whole area is shown covered with run-rig in 1806, and traces of these cultivation strips can be seen all over the lush green pastures.

This is one of the most beautiful corners of Eigg and one of the few places where the grandeur of the rugged scenery gives way to a more gentle landscape. Generations of islanders had chosen well when they made their homes at Grulin, until finally, this long continuity of settlement was broken when the last 14 families were forced to leave just over 130 years ago.

The 1870s were a time of relative prosperity for the island. Potatoes were again grown for sale and cattle prices were rising; but continuous cropping of the arable land meant that fertility was declining. Lack of security of tenure also hindered agricultural progress. Isabella, a daughter of Hugh MacPherson, continued to spend much time on the island and she was responsible for planting woodland in the south and stocking the high lochs with trout.

The Presbyterian church was built in the early 1860s, but improved in 1873. Before this the services had been held in the school room. After

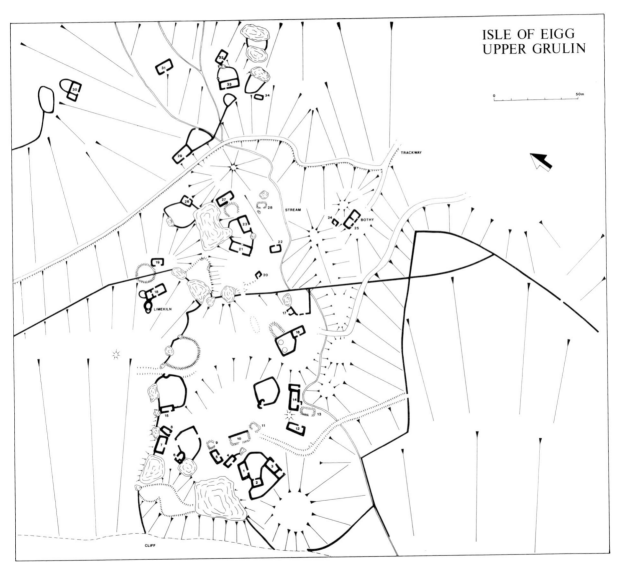

The 1986 survey of Upper Grulin. Some buildings are grouped around yards (21 & 23, and 1,2 3), while others are single buildings within a walled enclosure (15,6,16 & 28). All the buildings are round-cornered with central doors. Only number 30 and the bothy still in use have internal divisions. More houses are shown on the modern survey than on Bald's map; perhaps some of the buildings shown here were already ruinous by 1806.

bitter arguments within the Church of Scotland, it finally split at the 'Disruption' of 1844, with the evangelical group being ejected from the established episcopal church. The Rev Swanson was dispossesed of the Protestant living of Eigg, but undeterred he took up residence on his yacht, 'The Betsey', where he printed evangelical tracts for distribution throughout the Small Isles. He came ashore regularly and took services in a cottage. The Catholics had worshipped in a house at Kildonnan until 1810. Then the priest moved to Cleadale and services were held in the house where he lodged. The present chapel in Cleadale was built in 1910.

Educational facilities were variable. From 1812 the Gaelic School Society was setting up peripatetic schools that only remained in one place for between six and 18 months. They were enthusiastically attended in the Small Isles. The present school house was built in 1829, but the standard of teaching often left much to be desired. In 1836 the local clergyman wrote, 'The present schoolmaster is not noted for his attention to his scholars and often he has none,

the parents witholding them from school, knowing that they make no progress in their education under him.'

It was still difficult to keep children in school in the 1900s, when the school log book records numerous excuses for absence of which stormy weather is one of the most frequent. Sometimes when there had been a particularly long spell of bad weather, there was Saturday school to make up for lost time. Farm work, particularly potato planting and harvesting also kept children away. On October 30th, 1908, for instance, the log book records, 'Most of the crofters now have all their potatoes lifted, so children are able to come to school.'

Illness was also an important reason for absence. From January 21st to March 16th 1908, the school was closed due to an outbreak of measles; influenza and diptheria are also frequently mentioned as reasons for closure. In 1914 the school was closed for a fortnight as a result of diptheria when one child died. The school would also be closed for the day for events effecting the whole community such as

The schoolhouse in the early 1950s with children playing. The lad on the right in the kilt is Norman Jamieson who was the factor's son.

weddings and funerals.

Various incentives were introduced to get children to school. Attendance cards were given to those who went regularly. At one time those children who were present every day in the week were allowed home half an hour early on Friday. In the cold and stormy weather, children were sometimes given cocoa and a biscuit mid-day, and in the winter the school did not open until 10a.m. A visitor to the Lodge in 1908 left shillings at the school to be given to the best boy and best girl, but despite all these efforts, attendance remained difficult to enforce until the 1930s.

One problem was that many of the teachers did not stay long because they came from the south and did not understand island conditions. In 1908, the Inspector's annual report stated 'The controversy between the parents and the teachers during the past year and the bad attendance have militated against the efficiency of the school.' One of the main disagreements was over the use of Gaelic in the schools which was favoured by the parents, but not by the education authorities. The Inspector's report went on to say, 'It is quite evident also that far too much use has been made of the vernacular in the teaching of the children.' Often, however, teachers were dedicated and made great efforts to find places for able children at high schools on the mainland to continue their education.

The problem of getting good teachers at even smaller schools, such as the 'sub-school' on Muck, was much greater, and in 1920 the

A drawing from a photograph taken about 1900 showing the estate shepherd, Duncan Ferguson with his two small children.

teacher there was sacked because of the lack of achievement of her six pupils. They were 'unsatisfactory in all subjects'. However, a year later the situation had improved. The new teacher had brought up the school from 'one of the worst to one of the best'.

The numbers in the school up to the 1930s were usually between 30 and 40. Since then, as they have not been above 20, there has only been one teacher. When there were two, one would be Roman Catholic and the other Protestant. School assemblies would be separate, but otherwise the children would be taught together. Each church had its own religious festivals and there would be days when all the children of one denomination would be absent for religious reasons.

Great emphasis was always placed on singing in the school and the standard achieved was always commented upon favourably by the Inspectors. Gradually, the equipment in the school was improved and the value of education became generally accepted by the community.

Living conditions for the crofters were also improving. New building techniques began to be adopted from about 1820. Houses with square corners and chimney stacks in the gable walls began to be erected, the earliest of these being along the Low Road in Cleadale (NM476887).

Upper floors were probably not added until the end of the 19th century.

An important source of money for improvement was always that sent home by children and relatives working on the mainland or abroad. One new croft house overlooking Laig Bay was built in the last years of the 19th century with money made in the Yukon gold fields (NM475890). The old house was until recently used as a cow byre and the new house stands out as being of far more substantial build than the others in Cleadale.

Improved conditions were partly the result of a declining population which had dropped from 546 in 1841 to 282 in 1871. It rose slightly over the next ten years, but the number of occupied houses remained at 51. By 1881 there were very few cottars, or landless families left on the island and these were elderly and mostly single. The large farms employed farm labourers and servants, but otherwise all the families in Galmisdale and Cleadale were crofters; many combined crofting with another activity such as fishing, boat building or shepherding. Others are described in the 1881 census as a mason, seaman, merchant, and a cab driver. Shoes were also made on the island, but, as there were not enough trees to provide bark for tanning, the

Looking across to singing sands bay.

root of tormentil was used, which also dyed the leather a reddish colour. The gathering of enough roots was however, a long and laborious task. By the 1880s there was a post office at Galmisdale and women were finding employment as dress makers and tailors. None are described as weavers, although there was some domestic weaving, mostly for blankets, in Cleadale until the end of the century.

The remains of a croft where work on the land was combined with boat building and fishing can be seen on the cliffs overlooking Laig bay at Cleadale (NM471891). From here a good roadway runs down to the sea where a harbour has been painstakingly cleared by moving boulders off a small piece of shore. A saw pit is shown on the 1880 map near the harbour, and above, on either side of a stream was a small group of buildings. The remains of a lime kiln near the house shows that lime was burnt here. All the buildings are now ruined, but the one round-cornered house had a turf and rush thatched roof and a central fire until it ceased to be occupied in

the 1930s. It was the last such house to survive on the island. The roof was thatched with rushes laid on peat turves and had to be replaced every other year. Barns continued to be thatched in this way until more recently, but here too corrugated iron finally took over.

In 1881 the large farms at Laig, Sandavore and Kildonnan, were all tenanted by farmers from outside. Kildonnan covered 2,000 acres, 200 of which were arable, and was farmed by Walter Macfarlane from Glasgow. He employed three men, two women and two boys. Laig farm covered 2,675 acres of which only 68 were arable, and MacRae employed four men and one woman. Other outsiders on the island were the shepherds, the school teacher and the minister.

The 1880s brought more years of depression. The whole of agricultural Britain was suffering from a fall in prices as a result of foreign competition, particularly from the New World. Wool prices collapsed and so sheep farms were given up. Roderick MacRae left Laig and Peter Cameron from Ayrshire came with Ayrshire

Photograph taken immediately prior to the demolition of the priest's house in 1910 in preparation for the erection of the present house and chapel. The house, along with its croft, had been held by the priest since 1810 and was probably that built by Ronald Macdonald of Laig for his daughter in the 1780s.

Derelict agricultural machinery by the pier

cows. He used the milk for making butter and cheese, most of which he sold on the mainland. Potato blight was again hitting the crofters' crops and the decline in the fishing fleet meant that there was little chance of seasonal employment away from the island. Many land-owners throughout the Highlands saw the only chance to make profits was to exploit the great craze for deer stalking, and so wanted to let their land as deer parks. The eviction of the crofters began once again. This resulted in violence and riots, particularly on Skye. A parliamentary lobby supporting the crofters grew, and in 1883 a Royal Commission under Lord Napier was set up to investigate the conditions of the crofters. The commissioners travelled over most of the crofting areas of the Highlands and Islands, but do not seem to have taken evidence on Eigg, except to note that there were 28 crofters on the island making their living on between three and five acres each, plus their share of the common grazing on which they had the right to graze three cows and their progeny. In fact the number of cows varied from croft to croft and usually it was only the horses that were kept on the common grazing, the cows being kept on the croft.

The commissioners found much evidence for poverty and poor living conditions. In Lewis, for instance, there were still houses where the cow byre was not separated from the crofter's living area. The crofters themselves came in for much criticism. Remarks such as 'We were impressed by the unfavourable conditions in which the people live and their inability and reluctance to help themselves', are common. The main problem, which does not always seem to have been appreciated by the commissioners was that although there was not enough work to occupy the crofters all the year round on their crofts, there was little alternative seasonal work available. 'They pass much of their time in idleness. There is little or no demand for hired labour in their own neighbourhood and little disposition to work elsewhere. One of us was able to offer a large number of men employment in Glasgow for 20 to 25 shillings a week and at a season of the year that would not have interfered with their ordinary pursuits. It was on very rare occasions that men were willing either to accept the offer themselves or to recommend it to others. Unable to obtain profitable employment at home, they have grown up to manhood amidst a tradition opposed to continuous and laborious exertion.'

Many felt that there should be a potential for the expansion of the west coast fishing fleet, but the stormy nature of the sea and the lack of

Beech hedge: Galmisdale

harbours made this difficult; some men did travel to the east coast for the herring fishing in the summer.

In spite of these unsympathetic remarks, the Commission did come out in favour of giving crofters security of tenure, access to a court to determine fair rents, and the right to receive compensation for improvements made. The Crofters' (Scotland) Holdings Act embodying these recommendations became law in 1886.

In the 1890s the MacPherson family sold Eigg and it was bought by Robert Thompson. His wealth, made by selling armaments overseas, helped Eigg to prosper. He built Eigg Lodge where he lived from 1898 and carried out improvements to the property on his estate.

The building of the Lodge involved the last compulsory clearances on the island. There were ten households and 49 people at Galmisdale in 1891 and most of these were moved to new crofts at Chuagach, south of Cleadale. The boundary wall around the Lodge grounds was built with stones from the deserted crofts, so that little of them remains. Thompson provided the island with its first motor boat ferry, while farming was improved by the factor at Kildonnan. Thompson died in 1913 and was buried at the highest point on Castle Island. Eigg was then sold again, to Sir William Peterson,

who was only interested in the shooting. The cabinet minister, Sir Walter Runciman, bought the island in 1926 and it stayed in his family until 1966. Much was done to improve conditions. The Lodge was rebuilt in 1930 and a community hall erected in the grounds on the site of the old one. A warehouse and tea room were built at the pier and forestry developed. Since then Eigg has had several owners, none of whom has really been able to get to grips with the problems of the island's declining economy and dwindling population.

In conclusion, it can be seen that island life changed more quickly in the hundred years after 1800 than it had for many centuries before. Firstly the communal townships disappeared and the islanders became holders of individual small crofts. Conditions were aggravated by the rapid rise in population which was never below 450 in the first half of the 19th century and then the collapse of the kelp industry in the 1820s.

After 1841 the population began to decline and slowly, living conditions improved and farming techniques changed. The disastrous shift from cereals to potatoes began in the 18th century. The island was said to have no mill in 1811, (although one is marked on Bald's map) and corn was sent to Arisaig to be milled. Certainly by 1841 there was a miller again at Kildonnan and

A puffer at the pier unloading building materials for the Lodge c. 1930

Harvesting oats.

this water mill worked until the 1890s. By this time there was very little corn grown and instead sacks of flour were imported from the mainland. Although hand quern stones are sometimes dug up on the island, they have not been used for many centuries.

Throughout the second half of the 19th century, there were the usual variety of crafts practised within the small communities of the time. Shoe-makers, tailors, carpenters, a miller and a merchant are all mentioned. The tailor from Eigg travelled around the neighbouring islands making up locally produced cloth. It cost one pound to have a suit made, plus the tailor's board while he was making it. There was no post office until 1880, but a grocer is listed in 1861. There was a boat builder on Eigg throughout the period.

The list of occupations in the 19th century censuses suggests a community with a healthy variation of occupations, no more than the usual number of poor and a good proportion of the population of school age. However, this situation has changed greatly in this century as the population has continued to decline. Things are very different from 1841, when half the male population was under 20 years of age.

THE CROFTING COMMUNITY

Cow on the common grazing at Cleadale

By 1806, as William Bald's map shows, there were three distinct communities farming the fertile coastal plain of Cleadale on which there was hardly a flat area not covered by run-rig fields. The Roman Catholic church now stands on the site of the small farm created by Angus Macdonald of Laig for his daughter and son-in-law. The settlement of Cleadale itself was a little to the north, roughly where the modern road now divides.

Slightly further north, between the upper and lower roads, was Iltaig, about the same size as Cleadale. Further north still, beyond the present crofting area and just to the north of Howlin was Five Pennies. Although all signs of the original Cleadale and Iltaig were obliterated when the crofts were laid out in 1810, the ruins of the 16 houses at Five Pennies can still be seen today just as they appeared on Bald's map.

The setting up of the crofts involved a complete reorganisation of the land previously occupied by the townships of Cleadale and Iltaig. The 20 or so buildings on Bald's map in this area and the run-rig associated with them, were swept away and replaced by 17 crofts with straight boundary walls running up the hillsides behind the houses. The irregularity of the land meant that crofts varied considerably in size and shape and some were definitely better than others. The individual crofts were each capable of carrying three to five cows; in addition, there was a piece of common grazing to the north. This area has not been ploughed since 1810 and here the parallel ridges of run-rig contemporary with the old settlements can be seen especially in the low sunlight of dawn and dusk (NM4789). Each crofter was allowed one horse and these were kept on the common grazing. Unlike the huge Clydesdale horses kept by the estate, small Hebridean garrons, (a Clydesdale cross) were kept by the crofters. Originally, there were few horses on the island; strip fields and lazy beds were worked by hand using a traditional 'caschrom', or crooked spade. Agriculturalists who visited the island at this time thought there could be no improvement in farming until some modern implements were introduced, but recognised the value of the caschrom in working ground that was either too boggy or too stony for a horse drawn plough. By the time of the Crofters' Commission in 1883, most crofts had a horse which could be used for transport or for farm work. The only croft without a horse was the chapel croft: the priest did not need one as his land was worked for him by the crofters. By 1965, there were only two working horses in Cleadale, and when they were replaced by tractors the cows moved to the common grazing where they can be seen today.

Crops of potatoes followed by oats would be grown on the crofts. The oats would be undersown with grass and the land would revert to pasture for several years before being ploughed again. Oats was an important winter feed for cattle as well as horses and the potatoes were the staple food for the crofters. This was supplemented by rabbit and fish (every crofter had a boat); the fish would be salted down for the winter. A mixture of fish brine and mushy potatoes was considered a very good food for young stock.

Not until after the arrival of the Runcimans in 1926 were crofters allowed to keep sheep. Previous owners had been afraid that this would encourage sheep stealing and even then, crofters were only allowed two each. These too would be killed and salted down for domestic consumption.

Peat was an important source of fuel for crofters and the remains of their diggings can be seen above Cleadale on Beinn Bhuidhe as well as on the moorland between Laig and An Sgurr. Digging peat was hard work; the many cool springs along the cliff were kept free of watercress and other vegetation by passers-by so there was always clear water for those who needed a drink.

In 1898 Cleadale became the only crofting area on the island when crofters were moved from Galmisdale to Chuagach. Five equal crofts were established with about 24 acres each. The land was in five long narrow strips running down from the cliffs to the beach. The three shortest crofts were the southernmost and so they had some extra land in a triangular piece across the burn. Although very wet now, when the ditches were kept cleaned out each year, this was good arable land and far better than the Galmisdale crofts they had left behind. Common grazing for Chuagach was on Chleith Mhor, on higher ground beside the road. After the extension of this common grazing in 1919 to include an area to the west of the road as well, the grazing was about 140 acres; much larger than that for the Cleadale crofters but the land here was much poorer. Each of these crofts was allowed four cows and one horse. Sadly all the common grazing for the Chugach crofts has degenerated into bracken-covered moor.

During the 1914-18 war some new land north of the Cleadale common grazing was ploughed up as part of the war effort and good crops of

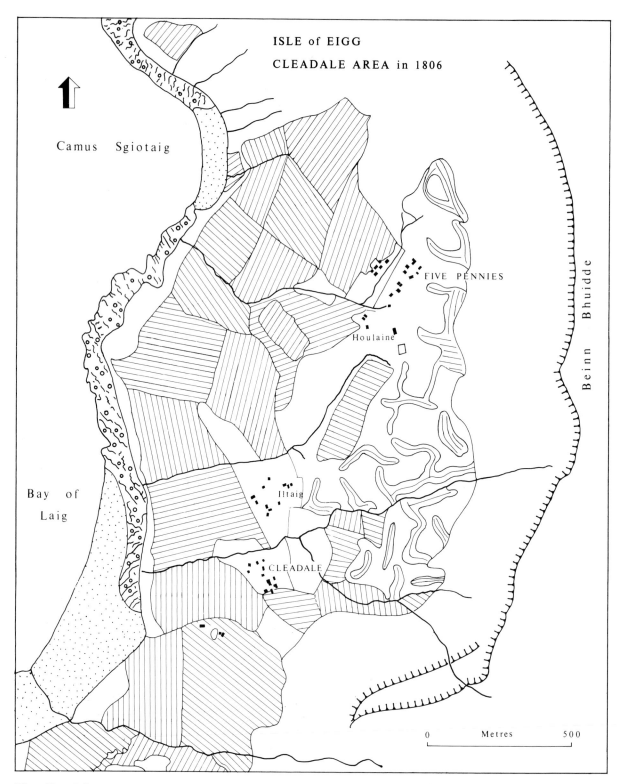

ISLE of EIGG

CLEADALE AREA in 1806

Camus Sgiotaig

Bay of
Laig

FIVE PENNIES

Houlaine

Iltaig

CLEADALE

Beinn Bhuidde

0   Metres   500

The Cleadale area in 1806 showing the separate settlements of Five Pennies, Howlin, Iltaig and Cleadale within their run-rig fields. The foundations of the houses at Five Pennies can still be seen.

oats were produced. In 1919 this land was added to the grazing, bringing the area there up to 110 acres. The estate paid for the original fencing around this new area, but it was up to the crofters to repair the wire. This fence is no longer maintained and estate sheep run freely over the common grazing while the crofters' cattle can now wander around the estate land at Howlin.

Living conditions gradually improved during the 19th century. Houses shared by animals and people were almost unknown by 1900, although up to 1918 in one croft house, that of Donald Robertson (croft no.17 on the map), cows and the horse, with the hens roosting above, shared the same roof with both animals and humans using the same front door. Donald himself spent the last 16 years of is life in bed having broken his leg whilst collecting drift wood on the singing sands.

The livestock were normally wintered, tethered in byres and if the winter was followed by a very bad summer they never went out. Although the small black Galloway cows that were kept were fairly hardy, it was easier to milk them indoors; while land was still cultivated the collection of manure was important. As land went out of cultivation in the 1960s and hardier Highland cross cattle were introduced cattle began to be out-wintered for the first time.

As well as manure from the byres, seaweed was spread on the land and rights to gather seaweed from particular stretches of the beach were jealously guarded. The acid soils also needed lime and the circular remains of several lime kilns can be seen in Cleadale.

The changes in the last 40 years on the islands have been more far reaching than any of the earlier enforced clearances. The departure of the young seeking greater variety and opportunities on the mainland has resulted in a drop in the population of Eigg from just over 200 in 1900 to barely 60 today. The crofting system has now virtually collapsed and it is difficult now to imagine the overcrowding of the 1840s when all the areas of remote lazy beds were cultivated and every available bit of flat land, however inaccessible, was planted for potatoes. This silent landscape where rushes and bracken are spreading and boundary walls crumbling, was once a busy place with fields filled with working people. Land had to be ploughed, oats and potatoes sown, weeded and harvested and hay made. Until the last war, all the crofts were worked and cultivated, but the decline in crofting began with the First World War. The loss of ten young men out of a total population of 200 was a devastating blow. Many others who left the island as soldiers did not return. Hugh MacKinnon of Eigg, described in a Gaelic poem:

Photograph of a crofthouse between the wars. The land is ploughed right up to the back of the house and the boat (every crofter had a boat) is pulled up to the gate.

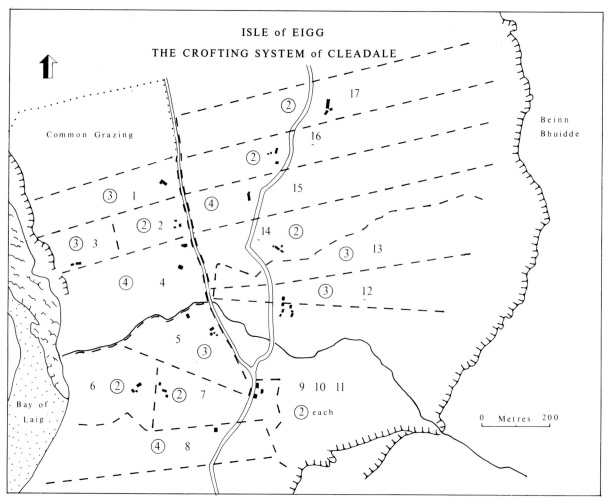

ISLE of EIGG
THE CROFTING SYSTEM of CLEADALE

The crofts in Cleadale laid out in 1810 that replaced the communal township. The boundaries shown here as dashed lines are those of the early years of this century. The crofts are numbered 1 to 17. The number of cows allowed on each croft in 1950 is indicated by the circled number in each holding and has not changed since the 1883 Napier Commission.

'How they went away wearing tartan
When the Kaiser struck his blow
And how they went away and did not come back.'

Younger members of the families had always gone away to seek work, either in highland regiments, the navy or as itinerant workers. The respect that Highlanders developed for education encouraged many to enter the professions. Previously, however, the attachment which this younger generation had felt for the small patches of land on which their grandfathers' had worked so hard ensured that family ties remained: those who moved away sent money home and when their help was finally needed on the croft, at least one member of the family would return. As the gap between the limitations of island life and the opportunities of the mainland became wider, fewer young people came back; the crofting community became not only a dwindling community but an ageing one. Gradually the traditional crofting system has been abandoned. Oats and potatoes had gone out of general cultivation by the 1960s and instead most of the land is used for grass. Cattle were the traditional export of the crofters and a few are still kept, but their numbers have declined. There are only two or three milking cows, and the suckler herd on the common grazing is mostly owned by one crofter. Until the 1940s it was worth the while of cattle dealers and drovers to come across to Eigg from Arisaig in the spring, and there would be an auction at which up to 40 overwintered store cattle might be sold. The sale was held on the flat land near the cattle grid above the pier (NM479839). Sometimes the drovers even went round the crofts buying direct. They came for a few years after the war, but as the cattle declined in number, they came no longer.

The Cleadale crofts from the Finger.   The upper and lower roads shown on the map can be seen with the crofts beside them.

This decline was obvious as early as 1955 when F.Fraser Darling in his West Highland Survey wrote, 'This basalt island is one of high potential fertility which has been allowed to go almost to dereliction . . .most of the Eigg crofters are now elderly and the future of the island as a crofting community is precarious . . .bracken is all too prevalent . . . the construction of a proper harbour would make it reasonably possible for the high potential of this favoured island to be reached. Without it, there is no hope.'

Little has changed for the better over the last 30 years. No adequate harbour has been constructed and year by year the costs of getting produce off the island increases while the self-sufficiency of the island decreases. Economies of scale make the import of mass-produced foods more attractive. Long-life milk and sliced bread are now the basic essentials for the islander rather than a house cow and a potato patch.

The reasons for this change are complex,but it is part of the general decline in small farms, particularly in upland areas, which has been accelerated by Britain's membership of the E.E.C. In 1950, for instance, a British dairy farmer could make his living from 15 cows. To earn the same real income he now needs 75; adaption on this scale cannot easily be made on the islands. In the last ten years the profits of large-scale cereal farming have so outstripped those of livestock that hill farming can only survive with the help of subsidies. The number of cattle kept in the Western Isles went down by 23% between 1976 and 1981. Prices for upland cattle, which are hardier and smaller are not keeping up with average trends. Crofts were never designed to provide full-time employment, yet now there is very little alternative work available. Encouragement is given through the Integrated Development Programme for the transfer of under-used croft land into the hands of the more active members of the crofting community. Other schemes such as community farming are possible and receive the backing of the Highlands and Islands Development Board. Autumn storms can still prevent stock being taken off for the sales at Oban; if they have to remain on the island the problems and expense of over-wintering make the whole enterprise unprofitable. All this is very disheartening to those who still presevere with island life.

Plough, telegraph hut and Askival

Not only are the crofts small; they are remote. As communications on the mainland become easier, the disadvantages of the islands become more obvious. The need for a deep harbour at Eigg was recognised as early as 1880 by the Napier Commission.

If the population continues to decline and land continues to go out of cultivation, the stage will soon be reached when the community is too small to support itself. It is usually the young people who have left, and although some younger families have moved in from outside, the problem of keeping the small ageing community going falls to a few active members. The school, with under ten pupils is not the same focal point that it was, when every family had a child there. With the lack of regular church services and the end of resident clergy in the 1950s, another focal point has been lost. Gone are the days when after mass and lunch, the families of Cleadale would gather on the cliffs overlooking the singing sands on a fine Sunday afternoon to talk over local affairs. All that is left is a regular ceilidh where recorded and sometimes disco-music have partly replaced traditional tunes. If the community is to survive,

then numbers must not drop any lower, but how can people be persuaded to stay? Life is hard and profits are small. Anyone taking on a croft needs an alternative source of income. The continuous battle against wind, rain, rabbits and bracken which is essential to keep the land in cultivation wears down in time even the most indomitable spirit. In the past any relaxation would have meant starvation. Happily, those times are passed, but now a lethargy can easily take over: once land has been neglected, it can be very difficult to retrieve. Every year the bracken and rushes extend a little further.

There are those who blame the economic decline of the Highlands and Islands on the Gaelic peoples themselves. They point to the meek acceptance of the clearances here compared to the violence in Ireland in similar circumstances. When the fight for the crofters' rights gathered momentum in the third quarter on the 19th century its success was due as much to the support of those who had already left the area but looked back nostalgically to their homeland as much as crofters themselves.

Tourism, craft industries and the arrival of people able to earn their living outside the region

UVS 100K

may help to keep a viable community on Eigg, but it is still the survival of its agriculture which is fundamental to the island's economy and landscape. Cattle must be kept on the land if it is not to disappear completely under bracken.

Land is a national resource and abandoned land is a sign of defeat. The time may come when agriculture will have gone full circle. The need for energy conservation, a drop in world prices and Common Market food surpluses may well reduce the viability of intensive farming; then, those areas which can produce good hardy stock

able to survive in a low input system could come into their own again.

In 1983 the E.E.C. recognised the Highlands and Islands as a 'severely disadvantaged region', which suffers exceptional problems as a result of remoteness, poor climate and unfavourable terrain. The net produce per hectare was calculated as 15% of the national average and they found that the number of livestock kept, especially cattle, was declining. Large sums of money were made available, initially for use in the Outer Hebrides, to develop agriculture,

Ploughed croftland awaiting the spring

fisheries, local industries and the infrastructure for such development.

It may be that 1987 will see the beginning of a change for the better. Efforts to drain some of the old crofting land at Cuagach have meant that every year a little more is ploughed and brought back into cultivation.

A weekly luncheon club for the over 60s has been set up with the help of local authority funds, but relying on the help of local local volunteers. Enthusiastic efforts are being made to raise the money need for a community hall in a more central position than the present one and there is interest in schemes for improvement.

Even those of us who love wild places know that abandoned farmland, like an abandoned garden soon becomes rank and waste and there is no charm in it. Farming here is the most difficult in Britain, and it is ironic that where there is so much in the rugged scenery to restore the soul, there are difficulties enough to break all but the most dogged spirit. It is with those very few armed with the strength of youth and the determination to keep traditions alive that the future of the island lies.

Community lunch for the seniors at the ceilidh hall

FUTHER READING

Banks, N., *Six Inner Hebrides* (David and Charles, Newton Abbot 1977)

Boswell, J., *Journal of a Tour in the Hebrides* (London 1773)

Campbell, J.L., *Canna, The Story of a Hebridean Island* (Oxford University Press, Oxford 1984)

Darling, F.F.et.al., *West Highland Survey* (Oxford University Press, Oxford 1955)

Grant, I.F., *Highland Folkways* (Routledge and Kegan Paul, London 1961)

Heron, R., *Scotland Delineated* (Edinburgh,1791)

Highland and Island Development Board, *Annual Reports*,1966-1985

Hunter, J., *The Making of the Crofting Community* (John Donald, Edinburgh 1976)

Kennedy-Fraser, M., and Macleod, Rev. K., *Songs of the Hebrides*, 3 vols.(Boosey and Hawkes London 2nd ed.1922)

Leigh, M., *Spade Among the Rushes* (Phoenix House, London 1950)

MacDonald, D.A.(ed), Hugh MacKinnon, *Tocher* 10 (School of Scottish Studies, Edinburgh 1973)

MacDonald, J., *A General View of the Agriculture of the Hebrides* (Edinburgh 1811)

MacEwen, L.A., *A Guide to Eigg and Muck* (Fort William 7th ed.1984)

Mackie, E.W., *Scotland, an Archaeological Guide* (Faber and Faber, London 1975)

MacPherson, N., 'Notes on the Antiquites of the Island of Eigg', *Proceedings of the Society of Antiquaries of Scotland*, (March 1878)

Martin, M., *A description of the Western Isles of Scotland* (1703, new ed. Stirling 1934)

Miller, H., *The Cruise of the Betsey* (Edinburgh 1858)

Robertson, Rev.C.M.,'Topography and Traditions of Eigg', *Proceedings of the Gaelic Society of Inverness*, Vol.22(1900)

Report of H.M. Commissioners of Enquiry into the conditions of Crofters and Cottars in the Highlands and Islands of Scotland (1884)

Sinclair, Sir J. (ed.) *The Statistical Account of Scotland* (Edinburgh 1791-8)

Storrie, M.C., 'A note on William Bald's map of Ardnamurchen and Sunart', *Scottish Studies* vol.5 (1961)

Wickham-Jones, C., & Pollock, D., *Rhum, the Excavations* (Edinburgh 1986)

Satellite TV comes to Cleadale 1987   *Back cover: Moidart from Eigg.*